D0214269

Protecting Main Street

Unlike other books which focus solely on the business or profit aspects of measuring the customer experience, this book focuses on the benefits to the consumer as well as the company or financial institution. The book describes how business and government can undertake market research to determine whether the credit and investment markets are functioning properly and providing consumers with adequate information to make sound and safe credit and investment decisions. A discussion of different market research methods abilities to uncover problems in the credit and investment markets is provided.

Findings and trends from studies measuring the customers experience in the credit and investment markets during the 1991–2009 time periods are discussed along with regulatory guidelines and consumer protection laws. The methodologies used to measure the customer experience and detect misleading sales practices, unfair treatment, and discrimination in the financial services market place are described in detail. The techniques of mystery shopping, matched pair testing, and consumer surveys are described along with a detailed discussion of study design, data collection methods, sample size determination, statistical testing, reporting, and analysis. Sample questionnaires, mystery shop scenarios and profiles, and sample analyses and charts are provided.

Paul C. Lubin has more than 30 years experience measuring and improving the customer experience. He owned and operated one of leading financial services market research firms in the country, Barry Leeds & Associates, and has worked for the leading financial institutions in America. He pioneered the use of market research to detect discrimination and unfair sales practices in consumer lending and developed self-testing testing programs for financial institutions facing allegations of discrimination and unfair sales practices.

Protecting Main Street

Measuring the Customer Experience in Financial Services for Business and Public Policy

Paul C. Lubin

NEW YORK AND LONDON

First published 2011
by Routledge
270 Madison Avenue, New York, NY 10016

Simultaneously published in the UK
by Routledge
2 Park Square, Milton Park, Abingdon, Oxon OX14 4RN

Routledge is an imprint of the Taylor & Francis Group, an informa business

Typeset in Minion by EvS Communication Networx, Inc.
Printed and bound in the United States of America on acid-free paper by Walsworth Publishing Company, Marceline, MO

Library of Congress Cataloging in Publication Data
Lubin, Paul C.
Protecting main street : measuring the customer experience in financial services for business and public policy / Paul C. Lubin.
p. cm.
1. Consumer credit—United States. 2. Mortgage loans—United States. 3. Bank loans—United States. 4. Financial institutions—Customer service. I. Title.
HG3756.U54L83 2011
332.1'70688—dc22
2010013767

ISBN13: 978-0-415-99601-3 (hbk)
ISBN13: 978-0-203-84198-3 (ebk)

For Mom

CONTENTS

LIST OF FIGURES

PREFACE

Buyer Beware and Dealing with Imperfect Markets

Unlike other books which focus solely on the business or profit aspects of measuring the customer experience, this book focuses on the benefits to the consumer as well as the company or financial institution. As such the applications of monitoring the customer experience are broader than helping a financial institution or any business improve revenues and customer retention by providing high quality service and products.

The applications of monitoring the customer experience include the formulation and setting of public policy and proper oversight of the consumer lending and the financial services marketplace to help ensure fair and reasonable treatment and sound financial decisions by consumers. The same monitoring programs verify sound business practices and help to ensure the optimal long term revenues and profits of financial institutions.

A precept of consumer protection is the assumption that the marketplace is the enforcement mechanism for preventing and correcting unfair and unsound business practices. The free flow of accurate and understandable information is critical. Given accurate, material, and understandable information, consumers make optimal decisions based on their best interests. Firms providing the highest quality and best value garner more customers and revenues. Consumers therefore police or weed out products and services that are faulty.

However, the information provided to consumers is not always understandable and is subject to imperfections and inconsistency, especially in the information gathering stage of a financial decision concerning products which by their very nature are complex.

Events in 2007, 2008, and 2009, namely the credit and liquidity crisis, housing crisis, consumer loan delinquencies and late payments, home foreclosures, and stock market crash point out the importance of proper monitoring of the consumer experience when dealing with lenders and providers of financial services. The absence of monitoring precludes the ability to discern whether the marketplace and an individual financial institution are providing consumers with the information and products needed to carry out decisions and transactions which optimize financial well-being and with it consumer wealth.

Customer experience monitoring gained increasing popularity in the mid- to late 1990s and their use by financial institutions and most businesses has accelerated into the new century. Service and product differentiation is recognized as critical to growth and profits, and its importance has been magnified by increased competition. Financial institutions view reliable measures of the customer experience as essential for determining whether or not they are meeting consumer needs. Government regulatory agencies in the early to late 1990s encouraged the use of these programs to assess adherence to regulatory guidelines and the law. These measurement programs aided financial institutions in managing risk by helping to ensure the optimization of revenue and profit by meeting customer needs. Customer experience measurement pointed out gaps in service and product offerings and helped identify changes necessary to ensure sound business practices.

At the turn of the 21st century a fundamental shift took place in the orientation of the government's role of ensuring that financial markets foster optimal consumer and business decisions. Oversight by the government and self-critical evaluation by financial institutions in the early to late 1990s was more intensive and focused than in the years between 2000 and 2009. Serious and focused regulatory oversight and enforcement was not needed to ensure fair treatment of consumers. Instead, it was deemed that the marketplace would serve as the enforcer of sound business practices and consumer protection. Consumers would elect to use those institutions with the best products and services and make decisions in their best interest. Regulatory oversight shifted focus to privacy, bank secrecy, and money laundering. There was a decline in the use of customer experience measurement as a tool to ensure sound, fair, and reasonable business practices. This shift in focus contributed to major disruptions in financial markets and more importantly household wealth and economic growth.

As the government changed its focus on oversight at the turn of the century so did financial institutions. Whether or not consumers were satisfied, would recommend those products, and would remain customers became more important than determining whether consumers were given accurate information and sold products that met their needs. Measures such as customer satisfaction, willingness to recommend, and likelihood to remain a customer became key performance metrics. Suppliers of these metrics gained business and these metrics also became sales tools. Increasingly, financial institutions and companies of all types touted their customer satisfaction ranking. A high customer satisfaction ranking attracted customers and reinforced the financial institution's image with consumers. However, whether consumers were being provided with accurate information and the information needed to make informed financial decisions was often neglected and instead financial institutions relied on a "buyer beware" philosophy. Consumers would judge whether or not they were provided with appropriate information and products to make optimal financial decisions. A "buyer beware" or "the marketplace as the protector of consumers" belief is particularly problematic in markets where products are complex, difficult to understand, where information does not flow freely, and where consumers are easily misled. Indeed these issues may have greater impact on consumers and households that are less familiar and comfortable with financial products, such as lower income households, first time home buyers, minorities, and immigrants.

Self-testing techniques in the form of traditional and time tested marketing research methods including mystery shopping, matched pair testing, and consumer surveys represent powerful tools for uncovering problems in business practices and policies in consumer lending and financial services.

The methods which have been used by government and business for decades can help detect and prevent unsound and unfair practices. For the consumer seeking credit and financial services products these problems may result in the inability to obtain information to make appropriate credit and financial decisions. For the financial institution it can result in unsafe business practices, discrimination, and misleading or unfair practices which in turn result in lost business, damage to reputation, and hefty financial penalties. For the nation these problems can result in inefficient and unsound financial markets where inappropriate decisions are made by the consumer and financial institution.

Customer experience measurement and self-testing can help assess whether the financial services markets are functioning properly for the consumer and they can serve to guide government policy and enforcement activities to ensure that the allocation of credit and purchase of financial products is based on sound sales, business, and underwriting practices that support the best long term interests of the consumer and the financial institution. For the financial institution, the techniques help limit risk and thereby foster profits by identifying and helping to correct problems in its sales and business practices.

Market research and self-testing over the last 20 years have shown changes in the financial marketplace that have affected consumers' ability to make optimal decisions. Such programs if conducted and acted upon continuously can help the nation build wealth by fostering a marketplace where consumers make appropriate decisions while financial institutions build customer loyalty and revenues.

1

CONSUMER LENDING AND SELF-TESTING

1.1 SELF-TESTING DEFINED

Self-testing is a voluntary undertaking that provides a critical window into the experience encountered by a consumer who purchases a product or conducts a transaction. When the financial institution measures the customer experience it is helped by ensuring adherence to business protocols and guidelines designed to satisfy customer needs and comply with government regulations and the law.

If the government is to develop and monitor the effects of public policy and determine whether financial institutions and the financial services sector are adhering to laws and guidelines intended to ensure efficient and fair markets, it needs to understand the experience customers encounter when they purchase a financial product (e.g., a mortgage loan, home equity loan, small business loan, credit card, or investment product). By measuring the customer experience, the financial institution as well as the government can help ensure that consumers are provided with the necessary information to make appropriate financial and credit decisions at every phase of the purchase process. This is vitally important from a business and public policy viewpoint. In the consumer credit market, for example, self-testing helps ensure compliance with a web of fair-lending rules and guidelines intended to ensure that minority and non-minority customers receive equal and fair treatment.

In light of laws, rules, and guidelines, overseen by the Federal Reserve, the Office of the Comptroller of the Currency, the Federal Deposit Insurance Corporation, the Office of Thrift Supervision, and other federal agencies, financial institutions and government agencies have developed and undertake monitoring techniques to assess the customer experience and detect whether customers are being treated fairly or unfairly, and if unfairly whether this is due to race, ethnicity, national origin, age, or gender.

1.2 THE IMPORTANCE OF SELF-TESTING FOR THE CONSUMER

Self-testing helps ensure that the consumer will receive the information required to make appropriate credit and financial decisions. Access to credit and financial products is critical to the economy. It enables consumers to more easily and quickly purchase fast moving products and services on a daily basis and purchase more expensive and capital intensive products such as a home, business, or automobile, or to finance education. All are critical to wealth and economic growth.

The consumer faces a myriad of credit and financial product alternatives. The consumer's ability to build assets is impaired if an individual chooses a credit product he or she cannot repay or makes the wrong choice of investment product. Many consumers do not have the knowledge to select the best product and rely on the advice of a financial institution. Given the complexity of credit and investment products the consumer can easily make decisions based on inadequate or misleading information.

Changes in the financial marketplace since the late 1990s have complicated an already difficult consumer decision process. A perfect example of this is the credit marketplace. Credit providers increased their product offerings, expanded sales channels, and accessed third parties to market their products and services. Technological advances enabled lenders to change the application process. Lenders can require the consumer to apply first, before the lender has provided information. Once the application is completed the lender can provide almost instant approval, thereby cutting short the consumer's search process and the period needed to gather information from multiple lenders and information sources. In fact the lender is motivated to cut the consumer's search process short in order to book the loan and generate revenues. When searching for a loan the consumer can choose from an even wider array of lenders and sales channels. The consumer can look toward his or her local bank, mortgage company, mortgage broker, finance company, sub-prime lender, credit card company, and investment company with a mortgage subsidiary. Indeed even a realtor can have a relationship with a mortgage company and can work with and refer the consumer to a lender. And then there are financial institutions that operate banks, mortgage companies, and finance companies all offering similar products but at different rates and terms. Depending upon the company or sales channel chosen the consumer can receive a variety of information and rates and terms. Gone is the day when a limited product set and information is provided through one or two types of financial institutions and delivery channels.

The increased number of financial products and credit products and delivery channels combined with greater reliance on third party relationships and sophisticated sales and marketing programs has created more risk for both the financial institution and the consumer. The financial institution is exposed to the business and legal risk associated with charges and allegations of unfair practices, discrimination, and violations of the law. The consumer faces the difficult job of choosing the right product. Choosing the wrong product may result in the consumer being unable to repay the loan or repaying a loan under less than optimal terms, both of which situations limit the individual's ability to build wealth. Choosing the wrong investment product can affect the consumer's current and future income as well as his or her financial security.

1.3 THE IMPORTANCE OF SELF-TESTING FOR THE FINANCIAL INSTITUTION

Self-testing helps the financial institution ensure that it is meeting consumer needs and verifies that its business practices are fair and sound and in compliance with the law and regulatory guidelines. Self-testing designed specifically to measure adherence to the law and regulatory guidelines (e.g., Fair Housing Act, Equal Credit Opportunity Act, Fair Trade Act, and Non-Deposit Investment Inter-Agency Guidelines and Rules of Fair Practice) also provides valuable information about the sales and service process and suggest areas where the financial institution can improve to better meet consumer needs. This in turn helps consumers make appropriate financial, credit, and investment decisions that build financial security for the consumer and the community.

By regular monitoring of consumer experiences, the financial institution can detect and resolve issues on a continuous basis. Ongoing monitoring helps detect potential and current violations of the law. It enables the financial institution to take action to resolve the issue before it results in complaints and allegations that can negatively impact reputation and sales. A plan that systematically tests sales and service practices is positively viewed by third parties, government regulators, and enforcement agencies. It is a pro-active step to help ensure that consumers are treated fairly and honestly. Hence it has been viewed as a mitigating factor by regulators and enforcement agencies when responding to complaints and when conducting investigations and reviews of lenders' and financial institutions' business practices. For the consumer it means a process that provides the information needed to choose the right loan at the most appropriate rates and terms.

The tests that have the specific objective of ensuring adherence to the Equal Credit Opportunity Act and Fair Housing Act are a good example of self-testing. The data or information generated through self-testing designed specifically to measure discrimination is privileged under the Equal Credit Opportunity Act (ECOA) and the Fair Housing Act (FHA). In order to encourage self-testing Congress in 1996 created a legal privilege for data gathered on a voluntary basis to specifically assess compliance with ECOA and the FHA. Government regulators defined self-testing as voluntary activities carried out by a third party that collect information assessing compliance that is not readily available or collected in a lender's loan files, applicant records, or through the lender's everyday normal business practices.

The self-testing privilege encouraged financial institutions to use more creative types of activities—mystery shopping, post-application surveys, and customer feedback—to help detect those issues that cannot readily be identified through reviews of customer loan files and on-site inspections by field auditors. Since then the definition of a self-test has been expanded to include activities to classify protected and non-protected classes of consumers applying for non-mortgage loan products in order to specifically assess compliance with ECOA.

Civil rights groups, community activists, government regulators, and enforcement agencies regularly use mystery shopping and post-application surveys to help detect violations of the law and to help guide and influence public policy. The HUD Matched Pair Testing program that assesses the treatment of minorities and non-minorities in the pre-application stage of the loan process is an example of this. In addition, HUD provides Fair Housing Initiative Program (FHIP) funds to community groups to test for discrimination in lending. And then there are the activist organizations, news organizations, and class action attorneys that use mystery shopping and other methods to test the sales practices of financial institutions.

1.4 PRO-ACTIVE SELF-TESTING

Ideally self-testing programs pro-actively seek to uncover (and correct) problems before they result in allegations of discrimination or unfair sales practices. However, many times financial institutions undertake self-testing as a response to a government enforcement or regulatory agency investigation or allegations of discrimination or misleading sales practices. The most effective approach is one that seeks to uncover (and correct) any deficiencies in marketing, sales, and service processes before they result in inappropriate credit and investment decisions, customer complaints, or allegations of unfair sales practices, discrimination, and referrals to regulatory authorities.

Too often a financial institution's orientation is not to be pro-active in terms of self-testing. Typical reasons for not being pro-active are: "We don't discriminate or mislead"; "Our business is to meet the consumers' financial needs; race does not play a factor"; "The consumer is responsible for his or her financial decisions; we don't mislead or force consumers to buy our products"; "The government is pressuring us to spend money to enforce social policy and aid groups perceived as disadvantaged. We all know why we are more careful with minorities; it's riskier to do business with them."

The most popular and accepted pro-active methods of self-testing are pre-application inquiries or mystery shops in the form of matched pair testing, triad testing, monadic testing, and post-application customer surveys.

2

SELF-TESTING METHODS TO MEASURE DISCRIMINATION, UNFAIR SALES PRACTICES, AND THE CUSTOMER EXPERIENCE

2.1 MYSTERY SHOPPING

One of the most frequently used approaches to measure the customer experience is mystery shopping, which calls for the use of testers or mystery shoppers who pose as potential or actual buyers. Unlike statistical procedures which require outcomes (loan approval, loan denial, account opening, pricing, etc.) and rely on abstract arguments and statistical principals, mystery shopping provides a record of the treatment or experience encountered by the mystery shopper or tester.

Mystery shopping has been used extensively to assess adherence to fair lending laws. The Equal Credit Opportunity Act prohibits discrimination on the basis of race, national origin, age, sex, marital status, and dependence on public assistance. The Fair Housing Act prohibits discrimination in mortgage lending based on the same factors plus religion, disability, and familial status. In tests for discrimination, a direct comparison of the experience encountered by protected mystery shoppers or testers and non-protected classes of mystery shoppers are made. For the most part self-tests have defined protected mystery shoppers as minorities, either African American or Hispanic and non-protected mystery shoppers or testers as non-minorities or Whites. At other times self-tests have been completed based on gender and protected testers have been females and non-protected testers have been males. Mystery shopping has also been used extensively to assess whether or not consumers are treated fairly, are not misled, and encounter reasonable lending practices when applying for credit.

2.2 MATCHED PAIR TESTING AND MONADIC TESTING

Matched pair testing and monadic testing are classic forms of self-testing used to detect discrimination in lending and unfair sales practices. The focus of matched pair testing is to determine the presence of disparate treatment in the pre-application stage of the loan process. Matched pair testing involves pairs of testers or mystery shoppers, minority and non-minority or male and female posing as potential borrowers or potential customers. Sometimes matched tests can comprise triads and what is termed sandwich tests. Triad tests comprise three testers, a control, normally the non-minority tester who is matched against two minorities (e.g., African American and Hispanic). A triad test design offers cost benefits in that a single control, a non-minority or White tester, is matched against two different test conditions, an African American tester and Hispanic tester. A sandwich test comprises two non-minority testers matched against one African American tester or one Hispanic tester. A sandwich test offers increased reliability by having two control conditions; for example, two White testers matched against a single test condition, such as a single minority tester. If the treatment of the two White testers is consistent and different from the treatment experienced by the minority tester then there is increased reliability of a true difference in treatment between the White testers and the minority tester.

The testers or mystery shoppers conduct their tests (shops) separately, but each is provided with profiles or scenarios. In most cases the profiles of the testers are very similar or matched. In some cases the minority tester takes on a slightly better profile than the non-minority, which increases the confidence that a difference in treatment between minority and non-minority testers is due to race or ethnic origin.

When testing for discrimination in lending, the profiles include the purpose of the loan (most often first time home buyer, though refinance, home equity/home improvement, and small business are also popular), loan amount, value and location of home, down payment, income and debt levels, rent as well as marital status. Profiles also include car rental and credit card payments, other loan payments, and the income of the tester and his or her spouse. When testing for discrimination and unfair sales practices in small business lending the profiles are more extensive and include the nature of the business, receivables, payables, other debts, sales, salaries, time in business and number of employees, in addition to loan amount and purpose.

The only significant difference between the profiles in a matched pair test is that one tester is a minority and one is not, or one tester is a male while the other is a female or one tester may be young while the other is old. Although a well-designed matched pair testing program can also provide information about service quality and sales professionalism, the specific objective is to evaluate and compare the treatment each tester receives and determine whether the treatment is equal.

Monadic testing reports the treatment encountered by one mystery shopper during one inquiry about a financial product. The focus of monadic testing is to detect patterns indicative of misleading sales practices and violations of the law, including section 5 of the FTC Act which prohibits unfair and deceptive practices and actions or patterns indicative of predatory lending. In addition, monadic testing may be used to detect violations of regulator guidelines; for example, Interagency Guidelines in the Sale of Non-Deposit Investment Products or the Financial Industry Regulatory Authority (FINRA) Rules of Fair Practice. Monadic testing has at times been used to detect discrimination and ensure compliance with fair lending laws, such as the Equal Credit Opportunity Act. When used in this manner the treatment of protected classes, for example, Blacks, is compared to the treatment encountered by Whites across different offices. The White testers and Black testers visit different offices. Enough offices are selected to represent the financial institution. Given a sufficient number of tests; for example, 100 tests or mystery shops conducted by White testers and 100 tests or mystery shops conducted by Black testers or mystery shoppers, significant differences in the treatment encountered by minority and non-minority testers can be identified. However the testing is less reliable than matched pair testing which calls for the minority and non-minority testers to visit the same office.

Self-testing, whether performed on a matched pair basis for fair lending or on a monadic basis for fair or reasonable treatment, can be conducted either in person or over the telephone. Most self-testing programs are conducted in person. However, consideration should be given to telephone based testing when consumers apply and conduct transactions over the telephone. Often lenders express concerns about testing for disparate treatment over the telephone. This author's experience as well as other studies[1] has shown that in many cases race can be accurately determined over the telephone.

Take the example of a mortgage company where representatives provided different treatment to minority and non-minority testers over the telephone. During discussions with a group of representatives selling mortgages over the telephone the representatives denied treating minorities differently. "We cannot tell the race or ethnicity of the caller over the telephone." Upon probing and asking if the representatives can tell the race of a Black associate in the room by the sound of his or her voice, the representatives respond they can tell the representative's race by the sound of the voice. Some representatives then go on to say it takes longer to explain mortgages to minorities and the loans are typically smaller, the next caller could be a jumbo, larger mortgage loan and the representatives' remuneration is based on the number of loans they book.

Evaluating representatives based on the number of loans booked resulted in rushing minorities off the telephone. Representatives judged they would book fewer loans and therefore make less money if they took the time needed to explain the loans to potential minority customers. This caused potential minority customers to receive less information than potential non-minority customers. The difference may be considered disparate treatment and a potential violation of the Equal Credit Opportunity Act and the Fair Housing Act.

2.3 POST-APPLICATION SURVEYS

Another form of self-test to ensure fair and equal treatment of consumers when applying for a loan is a consumer survey the author termed a post-application consumer survey in the early to mid-1990s. The consumer survey measures the information and assistance provided to consumers and their level of understanding of the terms and conditions of the loan or product purchased.

Post-application surveys as well as mystery shopping gained increasing popularity for the detection and prevention of discrimination in lending after the release of the Boston Federal Reserve's publications *Closing the Gap: A Guide to Equal Opportunity Lending* and *Mortgage Lending in Boston: Interpreting HMDA Data* (1992).[2] The Boston Federal Reserve's study of HMDA data found that race did play a role in the decision to approve or deny a mortgage loan.

The information obtained from post-application surveys and interviews with actual loan applicants can help determine whether the financial institution has provided a level of assistance that optimizes the opportunity for loan approval and whether the level of assistance is similar for minorities and non-minorities. The post-application consumer survey is particularly helpful for assessing the assistance and treatment provided to consumers for a variety of lending products, including home purchase mortgage, refinance, home equity and home improvement, unsecured or personal installment loans, auto and indirect loans, small business loans, and credit cards.

The post-application consumer survey measures the assistance and treatment encountered by actual customers (e.g., loan applicants or new customers). For example, loan applicants provide their assessment of the assistance and service received during the application and underwriting phases of the loan process. In self-tests designed to detect discrimination and whether consumers receive fair and equitable treatment, the experiences and perceptions of minorities, females, or older loan applicants are compared to the experiences and perceptions of non-minorities, males, or younger loan applicants.

Take the example of consumer surveys with loan applicants at a bank-owned mortgage company. While listening to telephone surveys among recent minority and non-minority mortgage loan applicants, only one group of loan applicants repeatedly mentioned they were waiting for an approval decision from the bank. That group comprised recent African American mortgage loan applicants. When evaluating the cause it was determined that two reviews of all minority applications were occurring, but no such policy was in place for non-minority applications. At the same time some surveys revealed that minorities were less likely to report being helped by a representative when completing the application. Non-minority mortgage loan applicants were more likely to report being offered flexible terms, the branch manager offering help to get the loan approved; and while non-minority applicants mentioned they applied at the branch, minority applicants were more likely to report being referred to the mortgage company. By conducting a second review of minority applications the bank attempted to ensure that loan approval decisions were correct. However, it delayed approval decisions and minority loan applicants were discouraged by the length of the process. In addition, the bank failed to recognize that it needed to police the assistance minorities received at the branches and whether or not it might be different from the assistance received by non-minorities. The bank thought its second review process sufficed to ensure fair and accurate loan decisions.

2.4 OTHER SELF-ASSESSMENT METHODS

Other popular tools used by lenders to measure the customer experience and help ensure compliance with laws and regulations are file reviews and statistical procedures (e.g., regression analysis). These tools are used heavily by compliance and fair lending departments at financial institutions. The objective is to verify adherence to fair lending laws and regulations by identifying disparate treatment of similarly situated protected and non-protected loan applicants. These tools are not classified as self-tests but are deemed self-assessments since they use information generated by everyday business processes. In contrast, self-tests, such as mystery shopping, matched pair testing, and post-application surveys produce information that is not normally available or produced by the company's business processes.

Regression analysis is used by financial institutions to help identify denied minority loan files that received a loan decision that differed from a similarly situated non-minority loan applicant. The financial institution then reviews the files involved and evaluates whether or not there were reasons for the difference and if the loan decision should be changed. Regression analysis is also used to help explain why pricing decisions are different for similarly situated protected and non-protected classes of consumers.

3
STEPS IN DESIGNING AND ANALYZING A SELF-TESTING PROGRAM

3.1 DEFINING THE PURPOSE

A clear definition of the purpose or objective of the self-testing program is vitally important to its success. A well defined objective includes guidelines concerning how the information will be used and the standard by which the information will be judged. An evaluation of different data collection methods is critical as well as the proper number of tests or surveys, tester profile and respondent definition, and questionnaire content.

A meeting between the designer of the self-testing program and the intended user of the information is mandatory. During this meeting the parties should define the issues and questions that need to be answered, standards upon which action will be taken, and when the information is needed.

The following sets forth the objective and action standard of many self-testing programs undertaken by financial institutions. The objective of the program is to determine the existence of disparate treatment of prospective loan applicants and client loan applicants on the basis of race or ethnic origin. The program will examine the following areas and non-minority and minority comparisons will be made (see Figure 3.1).

Disparate treatment will be judged based on the existence of statistical differences at the 95% confidence level between minority and non-minority testers and minority and non-minority loan applicants. Differences at the 80% confidence level will also be determined to help uncover a broader pattern of differences.

Self-Testing Information

Matched Pair Testing

- Detect disparate treatment
- Identify pre-screening and barriers to access
- Assess the extent and nature of suitability based questions
- Uncover income/credit skepticism
- Identify the information and terms provided and the products made available
- Identify product steering
- Detect selling without determining needs and ability to pay
- Identify disclosure of pertinent information needed to make appropriate credit decisions
- Detect omissions of costs, fees, terms
- Monitor unfair and misleading sales practices

Post-Application Consumer Survey

- Detect disparate treatment
- Identify whether access differs for protected classes
- Uncover assistance provided
- Determine whether assistance similarly maximizes the opportunity for loan approval
- Measure whether coaching and helpful advice occurs for non-minorities but not for minorities
- Assess the extent of determining needs and ability to repay
- Identify product steering
- Assess targeting of protected classes for inappropriate loans and frequent refinancing
- Measure disclosure and consumer understanding
- Measure customer satisfaction with the product and assistance provided

Figure 3.1 Self-Testing Information

It is important to define the action standard or the standard by which to identify disparate treatment. The purpose of the test is defeated if a less stringent standard is set. Take the example of a financial institution that undertakes self-testing and elects to complete 100 tests in total: 50 tests completed by White testers and 50 tests completed by Black testers. At the same time the financial institution is advised by legal counsel to only test for statistical differences at the 95% confidence level. Sixty-five percent of the time White testers are told they would qualify and 50% of the time Black testers are told they would qualify, a 15 percentage point difference. There is no statistically meaningful difference in the treatment of White and Black testers using the 95% confidence level. The bank determines it is treating potential White and Black loan customers the same and does not take action. Had the bank used the 80% confidence level, a difference between White and Black testers would have been identified and the bank could consider taking action to correct the situation. In this situation the bank was relatively assured it would not find statistically meaningful differences, given the small number of tests completed and the confidence level it used to test for statistical differences. Nevertheless, the financial institution informs its regulator that it conducts self-testing and earns credit from its regulator for doing so. Self-testing should be used as a mechanism to help prevent disparate treatment and ensure adherence to the law. Using a less stringent or loose action standard defeats the purpose of a self-test.

3.2 DESIGNING THE QUESTIONNAIRE

3.2.1 Designing the Mystery Shop Questionnaire

The design of a mystery shopping questionnaire for matched pair testing or monadic testing is different from the design of a post-application consumer survey. Unlike consumer surveys where the interviewer administers a survey with a consumer or respondent, the mystery shopper or interviewer is the respondent. And while a consumer survey reports the consumer's perception of what occurred, the mystery shopper records what actually happened. The mystery shopper is required to remember the experience and record the actions and information provided to him or her. As such the questionnaire needs to foster the mystery shopper's ability to accurately remember and record the experience.

The mystery shop questionnaire should ideally be easy to understand and easy to complete. The questionnaire should be in checklist (yes/no) form with subjective questions such as overall shopper satisfaction with the experience at the end of the questionnaire. This helps reduce bias associated with what the mystery shopper feels is important by keeping the mystery shopper focused on what happened during the mystery shop. Another big help is to ask the mystery shopper to write a detailed narrative of what occurred; the narrative should ideally follow the order of the experience but can also cover key points in the sales process. For example, in a mortgage loan questionnaire, the products discussed and its terms and fees should be described in detail by the mystery shopper. When the mystery shopper is required to write a narrative it provides an avenue for obtaining information that is not necessarily covered by the yes/no and rating questions in the questionnaire. A narrative is particularly helpful during editing. It can clarify and resolve ambiguous or conflicting information provided by the mystery shoppers or testers.

REQUIREMENTS FOR A BIAS FREE MYSTERY SHOP QUESTIONNAIRE

- Keep it easy to understand.
- Keep it short and concise.
- The bulk of questions should be objective, did it happen or not?
- Checklist, yes/no format.
- Order of questions should follow the sequence of the customer experience.
- Do not mix topics in one question. For example, whether the representative greeted you and shook hands are separate questions.
- Leave room for narrative by the shopper.
- Ask subjective questions or shopper ratings at the end of the questionnaire.
- Shopper takes notes during shop as a normal customer.
- Shopper completes the questionnaire immediately after the mystery shop.

Figures 3.2 and 3.3 are examples of narratives that may be included in a questionnaire.

The questionnaire should trace the flow of the sales and service process. This helps the mystery shopper remember the experience and accurately record details of the shop. For example, if a potential customer is most likely to be first greeted and referred to the appropriate representative, the questionnaire should first address the greeting

TESTER NARRATIVE—1

COMPLETE THIS SECTION BEFORE COMPLETING THE QUESTIONNAIRE.

I. Write a description (DESCRIBE THE EVENTS IN THE ORDER IN WHICH THEY TOOK PLACE) of your customer experience during the inquiry Include anything unusual that might have happened and your general impressions. (PLEASE PRINT)

Figure 3.2 Tester Narrative—1

TESTER NARRATIVE—2

PLEASE COMPLETE THIS SECTION PRIOR TO COMPLETING THE QUESTIONNAIRE.

Please provide a description of your customer experience concerning the following topics. Describe in detail. One word answers are not acceptable.

Describe the features and terms of all loans discussed (e.g., ARM, Interest Only, Fixed Rate, Low Documentation etc.).

Discuss the relative advantages and disadvantages of the products that were discussed.

Describe the questions asked by the representative.

Discuss the costs and fees of the loans that were quoted. Include all costs and fees (e.g., prepayment penalties and points).

Discuss escrow payments that were required.

Describe the documents required with loans.

Discuss the steps required in the application and approval process.

Describe the opinions provided about whether or not you would be approved for the loan.

Discuss the Interest rates and monthly payments that were quoted?

Describe anything unusual that might have happened and your general impressions.

Figure 3.3 Tester Narrative—2

and referral. If the next stages are determining needs, offering products, and finally summarizing the products and asking the potential customer about next steps, the questionnaire should cover these topics in the same order. Figure 3.4 lists sample questions for uncovering disparate treatment by measuring the experience encountered by matched minority and non-minority testers or mystery shoppers in the pre-application stage of the loan process.

SAMPLE QUESTIONS FOR A MATCHED PAIR TESTING QUESTIONNAIRE

1. **When you called the location, were you told to make an appointment, just come in, told to call back or were you referred to another financial institution?**
2. Did you wait? How long?
3. **Did the representative stand up to greet you, offer you a seat, ask for your name, use your name, make you feel important, hurry or rush you?**
4. Did the representative ask you the purpose of the loan, loan amount, value of home, location of the home, down payment amount, type of home, your income, debt, marital status, employment and length of employment and savings and investments?
5. **What was mentioned about your down payment? Were you told your down payment was adequate or falls short of approval standards?**
6. What mortgages were mentioned and recommended?
7. **Were you offered an opinion about whether or not you would qualify for the loan?**
8. Were you told you would probably qualify?
9. **Did the representative encourage you to apply?**
10. How long did the representative say it would take to find out if you were approved?
11. **Were you offered an application?**
12. Were you offered help to complete the application?
13. **Were told what information to provide with your application?**
14. What information were you told to provide?
15. **How satisfied were you with the overall service you received?**
16. Why?

Figure 3.4 Sample Questions for a Matched Pair Testing Questionnaire

3.2.2 Designing the Post-Application Questionnaire

The post-application questionnaire is administered over the telephone by an interviewer. Some of the basic tenets apply for designing a strong mystery shop questionnaire. The questionnaire should be easy to understand and complete and the questions should be objective and not lead the respondent. Survey length is also important, since it can affect accuracy. Unlike a mystery shopper who is familiar with and reviews the questionnaire before the mystery shop, the respondent does not know the questions. Survey length and questions that are difficult to understand can quickly lead to respondent fatigue and inaccurate responses or interview termination.

Question order should be carefully considered. Questions asked in the beginning of the survey can influence the answers provided to questions that follow. For example, a question regarding overall satisfaction with the service should be asked first. This ensures that the customer will consider only those factors which he or she deems important when evaluating overall service. Asking the customer to rate the financial institution on a series of attributes (e.g., assistance with completing the application and advice) before asking the customer for his or her overall satisfaction may cause the customer to consider these attributes when he or she might not normally do so. Another example of the effect of

REQUIREMENTS FOR A BIAS FREE CONSUMER SURVEY

- Keep it easy to understand.
- It should be as short as possible and easy to complete.
- The questions should not lead the respondent or customer. Don't start a question with stating a fact. For example, too often representatives do not mention the key features of a product. Did the representative clearly explain the product?
- Try to make the survey interesting.
- Carefully consider the order of the questions and if they can influence the answers to questions asked later in the questionnaire
- Consider the length of scales and whether they will be easy to answer. For example a 7-point scale may be more difficult for some customers to answer than a 5-point scale.
- Eliminate questions that collect the same information and therefore lengthen the questionnaire

question order is asking likes before dislikes. All too often asking likes before dislikes seems natural and more comfortable. But when consumers are first pressed to offer what they like about service they are more reluctant to express what they dislike. Asking about dislikes before likes requires the customer to think about anything that caused discomfort and therefore provides the financial institution with more information about how to improve its service and the nature of the service provided to protected and non-protected classes of customers.

The questionnaire should cover the following areas in order to assess whether customers are being treated fairly and whether minorities and non-minorities and males and females are being treated similarly:

- Encouragement: Is the customer provided with a sense or likelihood of loan approval and does she or he receive a recommendation about a suitable loan and follow-up calls about loan status and problems?
- Creativity: Does the lender seek information about additional sources of income and the possibility of increased income, intent to pay down debt, and any gifts that can be used toward down payment?
- Quality of Assistance: Does the customer receive help completing the application and does he or she receive explanations about the terms and conditions of the loans offered as well as accurate information about the process and deadlines that need to be met? (see Figure 3.5)

3.3 DESIGNING THE MYSTERY SHOPPER OR TESTER PROFILES

Critical to the success of a matched pair or monadic testing program designed to detect discrimination or misleading sales practices is the tester profile, which contains the financial circumstances and needs of the tester and provides the tester with the information needed to answer questions.

The testers or mystery shoppers conduct their tests (shops) separately, but each is provided with a profile. In most cases the profiles of the testers are very similar or matched. In some cases the minority takes on a slightly better profile than the non-minority.

When testing the pre-application stage of the loan process the profile normally includes the purpose of the loan (most often first time home buyer, though refinance, home equity/home improvement, and small business are also popular), loan amount, value and location of home, down payment, income and debt levels, rent, as well as marital status. Profiles also include car and credit card payments, other loan payments,

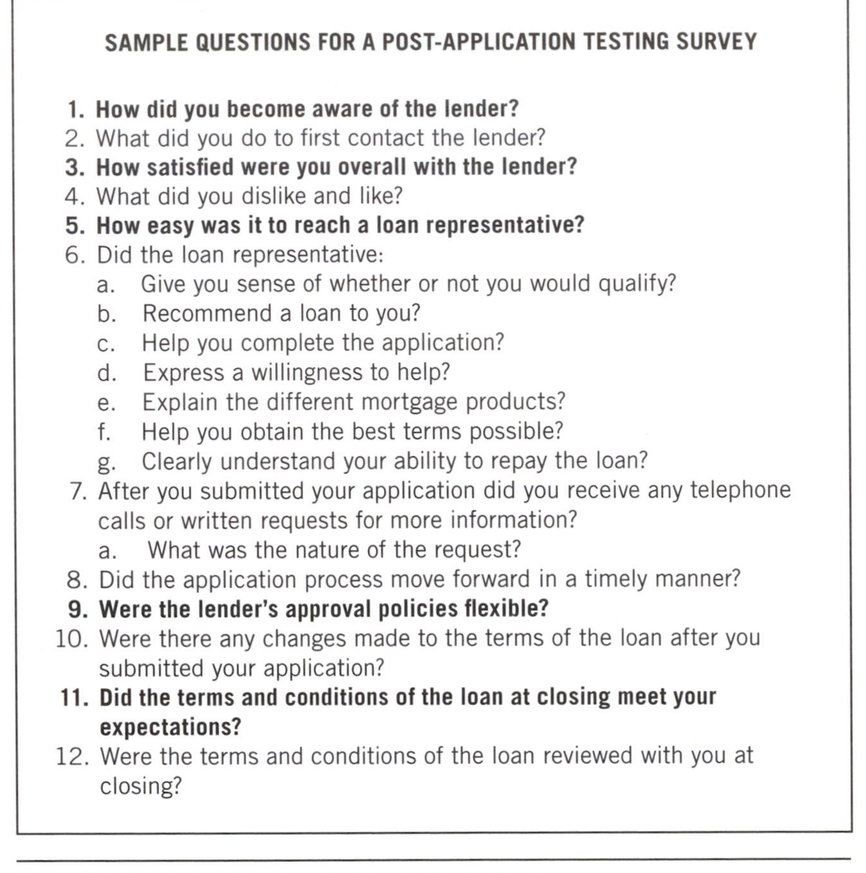

SAMPLE QUESTIONS FOR A POST-APPLICATION TESTING SURVEY

1. **How did you become aware of the lender?**
2. What did you do to first contact the lender?
3. **How satisfied were you overall with the lender?**
4. What did you dislike and like?
5. **How easy was it to reach a loan representative?**
6. Did the loan representative:
    a. Give you sense of whether or not you would qualify?
    b. Recommend a loan to you?
    c. Help you complete the application?
    d. Express a willingness to help?
    e. Explain the different mortgage products?
    f. Help you obtain the best terms possible?
    g. Clearly understand your ability to repay the loan?
7. After you submitted your application did you receive any telephone calls or written requests for more information?
    a. What was the nature of the request?
8. Did the application process move forward in a timely manner?
9. **Were the lender's approval policies flexible?**
10. Were there any changes made to the terms of the loan after you submitted your application?
11. **Did the terms and conditions of the loan at closing meet your expectations?**
12. Were the terms and conditions of the loan reviewed with you at closing?

Figure 3.5 Sample Questions for a Post-Application Testing Survey

and the income of the tester and his or her spouse. The only significant difference between the profiles in a match pair testing program is that one tester is a minority and one is not, or one tester is a male while the other is a female or one tester is young while the other is old.

In most tests to uncover discrimination, testers take on profiles which are marginal or just qualify for the loan based on the lender's underwriting guidelines. The intent here is to present a test condition that is more likely to draw out skepticism or preconceived notions about a minority's or a member of a protected class's ability to qualify for the loan. Other test profiles set conditions such that the protected class is slightly better qualified than the non-protected class. The tester or mystery shopper should not be told he or she does not qualify (see Figure 3.6).

THE TESTER PROFILE	
Mortgage Inquiry	
Home Information	
Purchase price	$300,000
Down payment	10%
Property tax	$4,000
Age of home	10 years
Debt Information	
Credit card	$150 per month
Car loan	$250 per month
Other debt	$100 per month
Rent	$600 per month
Income, Employment and Savings	
Yearly combined income	$100,000
Tester's income	$60,000
Spouse income	$40,000
Savings	$50,000
Tester occupation	Computer programmer
Spouse occupation	Administrative Assistant

Figure 3.6 The Tester Profile

3.4 DESIGNING THE SCENARIO

Crucial to the successful completion of a matched pair testing or monadic testing program is the scenario. Together with the profile, the scenario describes the inquiry and how testers approach the financial institution (see Figure 3.7). This ensures consistency in how each test is conducted and the financial institution reacts to the same test conditions. In the absence of the scenario the experience encountered by the tester may be affected by how the tester or shopper approached the financial institution. The scenario should describe how the tester first contacts the financial institution, for example, by walking into a branch or calling for an appointment, what the tester should first say, the questions he or she asks, and how the tester should reply to questions asked.

The Scenario

Mortgage Loan Inquiry

Walk-in the branch during your assigned day and time.

Notice the time you enter the office ("Time entered office") and the time you leave the office ("Time left office").

Approach any available representative and ask to see someone about a loan.

Keep track of the amount of time you spend waiting (if any) for the representative to become available to help you.

When you reach the representative who can help you with loan information, restate (if necessary) that you want some information about a mortgage. If he/she asks what kind of loan you are interested in, say:

"I'm not sure. I want to see what you have available."

If the Loan Officer asks you probing questions, respond as indicated in this scenario and in your Shopper Profile.

Listen carefully to everything the representative tells you about different types of loans. If you find it necessary to take notes, you may do so as a normal customer would.

Listen for any discussion of:

- features and/or benefits of loans
- closing costs
- interest rates
- approval time
- monthly payment
- opinion about qualification

Figure 3.7 The Scenario

If the representative did not provide the following information, you must ask:

An opinion about qualification:	Do you think I could get a loan?"
The monthly payment:	"What would my monthly payments be?"
The interest rate or APR:	"What is the interest rate?"
The closing costs:	"Are there any closing costs?" "How much are the closing costs?"
Approval Time:	"How long does it take to find out if I can get the loan?"

Answers to Other Questions

What is your name? Provide an alias

What is your social security number? "I will be glad to give out that information if I decide to apply, but right now I'm just trying to see what you have to offer."

What is your telephone number? "I will be glad to give out that information if I decide to apply, but right now I'm just trying to see what you have to offer."

Where do you bank? Cite your own bank

What length of a loan are you interested in? "I'm not sure. What do you have?

Do you want a fixed-rate loan or a variable-rate loan? "I'm not sure. What's available"

See your Shopper Profiles for specific information. You have a different profile for each office you are assigned to visit.

Upon completion of your inquiry, leave the office and drive away. Fill out the questionnaire after you are a few blocks away from the office. Staple the representative's business card to the questionnaire at the top in the center. Attach any brochures/materials received to the questionnaire.

Figure 3.7 Continued

3.5 THE ANALYTICAL APPROACH

3.5.1 Analyzing Matched Pair Testing and Monadic Testing Results

In matched pair testing, side-by-side analysis compares the experience encountered by a minority or protected class tester to the experience encountered by his or her non-minority or non-protected class counterpart. The experience of each of the minority testers and non-minority testers are aggregated and the total results compared to detect disparate treatment. In monadic testing the treatment of a single tester is evaluated one-off. The results for each of the tests are then aggregated. The evaluation detects whether the experience encountered by the testers adheres to the financial institution's policies, consumer protection laws, and applicable regulatory guidelines.

In a side-by-side review, the analyst compares the experiences recorded by the protected class testers (e.g., the Black testers) to the experiences recorded by the non-protected testers (e.g., the White testers). At times the analyst may need to debrief the testers in order to better understand the experience each tester encountered. Some matched pair testing programs call for debriefing testers immediately after completion. During the debriefing a test coordinator or supervisor interviews the two testers and completes the questionnaire. In other matched pair testing programs, the testers are debriefed in a focus group setting. One tester focus group comprises the protected class testers (minority, female, or older) and the other focus group comprises the non-protected class testers (non-minority, male, or younger). The typical size of the tester focus group is anywhere from four to eight testers. The focus group setting offers the advantage of debriefing several testers at the same time. The testers discuss and compare experiences and the financial institution can clarify answers during the discussion. The focus group session is normally recorded and excerpts used during presentation of results.

To aid in the side-by-side comparison, a computer tabulation program can be used. This is especially helpful when a large number of tests have been completed. The analyst can use the computer tabulation program to identify locations or offices where the experience of the minority tester differs from the experience encountered by the non-minority tester on critical key fair lending issues, such as: encouraged to apply, positive opinion offered about loan qualification, time spent with the tester, approval time, closing costs quoted, and loan recommended. The computer tabulation describes the treatment of the minority and non-minority testers at each of the branches or loan officers tested. Figure 3.8 graphically displays the report.

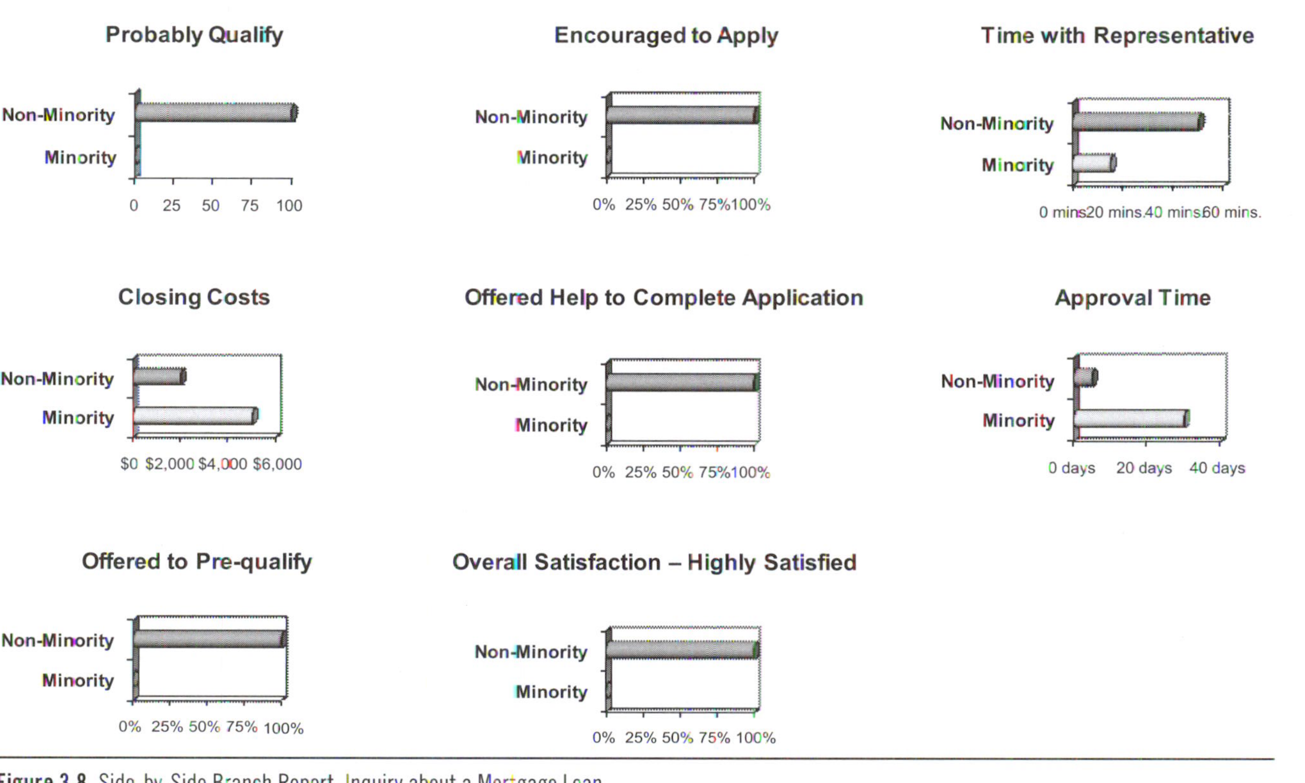

Figure 3.8 Side-by-Side Branch Report, Inquiry about a Mortgage Loan

At the corporate or national level, testing will help determine whether a pattern or practice exists of disparate treatment and misleading sales practices. A sufficient number of tests are required to determine whether a pattern or practice exists of treating minorities or protected classes differently from non-protected classes. Ideally, no less than 100 matched pair tests (or 100 minority tests and 100 non-minority tests) should be conducted by a financial institution with a large branch network. This provides a sufficient number of tests for statistical testing and reliability.

As a practical matter the number of tests is limited by the number of loan representatives and branches of a financial institution. A financial institution with 20 locations and eight loan offices would not want to undertake 100 matched pair tests. Conducting 100 matched pair tests would require multiple tests of loan officers or branches and would probably be detected by the personnel of the financial institution. In this situation the financial institution could complete 20 matched pairs (or 20 triad tests, non-minority, African American, and Hispanic) and test each of its branches. The financial institution might also decide just to test its loan officers and conduct eight matched pairs (or eight triad tests). The final number of tests should take into account the size of the population of potential customers inquiring about a loan as well as the number of branches and loan officers.

When reviewing results and comparing the treatment of minority and non-minority testers, tests of significance should be conducted at the 95% confidence level and the 80% confidence level. Conducting tests of significance at the 80% confidence enables a more rigid standard for asserting that non-minorities and minorities are treated similarly and there is no disparate treatment. Testing at the 80% confidence level enables the analyst to uncover more differences in treatment. For example, let's assume a mortgage lender conducts 100 matched pair tests or 100 minority tests and 100 non-minority tests. When reviewing the results the lender finds in Figure 3.9.

Based on t-tests and assuming 100 non-minority tests and 100 minority tests, only one behavior is statistically significant at the 95% confidence level, recommended a loan, as indicated by an asterisk. The other differences are all statistically different, indicated by a plus, at the 80% confidence level. Using only the 95% confidence level only one difference is identified, offering a loan recommendation more to non-minority testers. The analyst concludes there is no difference in treatment. Differences appear across all elements when the 80% confidence level is used. The analyst concludes a pattern favoring non-minority testers. Testing at the 80% confidence level is a more rigid standard for detecting a pattern of treating minorities differently than non-minorities.

SIDE-BY-SIDE LENDER DIFFERENCES

Matched Pair Testing

Matched Pair Testing	Non-Minority	Minority
Probably will qualify	50%+	40%
10% down payment is sufficient	60%+	50%
Offered application	70%+	60%
Offered help to complete the application	40%+	30%
Recommended a loan	90%*	75%
Informed about APR	80%+	70%
Told about documents required to apply	65%+	55%
Offered to schedule appointment to complete the application	45%+	35%
Discussed FHA Loan	50%	60%+

* Significant at the 95% confidence level
+ Significant at the 80% confidence level

Figure 3.9 Side-by-Side Lender Differences, Matched Pair Testing

3.5.2 Analyzing Post-Application Consumer Survey Results

In a post-application consumer survey results are reviewed in total and by minority and non-minority loan applicants or by loan applicants classified as protected and non-protected (e.g., minority and non-minority and female and male). The number of surveys completed needs to be sufficient to represent the population of applicants within each group. The number of surveys also needs to be sufficient to provide statistical reliability around which decisions will be made. When undertaking a post-application consumer survey to identify the existence of disparate treatment during the mortgage loan application process the analyst needs to specify a confidence level and action standard for deciding whether disparate treatment exists. Specifying a confidence level and action standard is crucial for determining an appropriate sample size or number of interviews.

For example, a lender wants to verify that the level of assistance it provides to minority and non-minority loan applicants is similar and of a nature that maximizes their opportunity for loan approval. As a first step it sets an action standard. The action standard states non-minority and minority loan applicants experience and receive different assistance if a statistical difference exists at the 95% confidence level.

In addition, a directional or more subtle difference will exist if the difference is significant at the 80% confidence level. The level of assistance will be measured based on overall satisfaction, assistance when completing the application, assistance during application processing, information provided about loans, loan terms and rates, timing and efficiency of the loan application process, and loan terms and rates at closing met expectations.

For example, 300 surveys are completed among minorities and 300 interviews are completed among non-minorities and 50% of non-minorities report receiving help or assistance when completing the application versus 40% of the minorities. In this example the difference is significant at the 95% confidence level and the finding is that non-minorities are receiving more help when completing a loan application than minorities.

When reviewing results and comparing the treatment of minority and non-minority loan applicants, tests of significance should be conducted at the 95% confidence level and the 80% confidence level. Similar to matched pair testing, conducting tests of significance at the 80% confidence is a more rigid standard for asserting non-minorities and minorities are treated similarly and there is no disparate treatment. Testing at the 80% confidence level enables the analyst to uncover more differences in treatment. A smaller difference is required between minorities and non-minorities to be deemed as significant.

For example, let's assume a mortgage lender completes 300 surveys with minority applicants (150 African American and 150 Hispanic) and 300 surveys with non-minority loan applicants. When reviewing the results the analyst finds the following significant differences at the 80% confidence level: lender is somewhat more likely to contact non-minorities to clarify information on the application and tell non-minorities about the information required for the application. In addition, non-minorities were somewhat more likely to report they received a sense about whether they would be approved, agree the bank has flexible loan standards, representatives spent an adequate amount of time, and informed them about the annual percentage rate. Non-minorities were also more likely to be highly satisfied with the service, report a loan was recommended, they received help in completing the application, representatives offered advice on how to improve the application, and asked about the probability of increased income in the future (see Figure 3.10).

In addition to reviewing results in total by non-minority and minority, the analyst should review results by race and ethnic status. For example, the experience and perceptions of African-Americans should

SIDE-BY-SIDE DIFFERENCES

Post-Application Consumer Survey

	Non-Minority	Minority
Extremely or vey satisfied overall with the service	58%*	50%
Received help when completing application	50%*	40%
Recommended a loan based on your needs	60%+	54%
Gave a sense of likely loan approval or not	75%+	69%
The lender spent an adequate amount of time with you	70%+	64%
Offered advice about how to improve your application	40%*	30%
Recommended a loan	90%*	75%
Informed about APR	80%+	75%
Told you about documents required with your application	65%+	59%
Received a call to clarify information on your application	45%+	39%
Asked about the probability of increased income in the future	60%*	50%
Flexible loan approval standards	50%+	44%

* Significant at the 95% confidence level
+ Significant at the 80% confidence level

Figure 3.10 Side-by-Side Differences, Post-Application Consumer Survey

be reviewed separately from Hispanics and Asians and compared to non-minorities. Similarly the analyst should account for gender and marital status. Other points to consider are the status of the application. Was it approved or denied? Was it withdrawn? It is important to interview minority applicants and non-minority applicants who were denied. It reveals whether non-minority denied applicants report greater assistance and coaching than minority denied applicants. If possible an equal number of interviews should be completed by minority and non-minority approved applicants as well as minority and non-minority denied applicants.

Similar to matched pair testing, the analysis compares the perceptions and experiences of minorities and non-minorities. The comparison is usually at the total or corporate level, though comparisons can be conducted by branch and loan officers. The same process is used in post-application consumer surveys to identify a pattern or practice of discrimination or misleading sales practices.

Differences in the treatment experienced by minorities or non-minorities are often subtle in nature. Testing for statistical differences between minorities and non-minorities provides a systematic way of determining whether differences exist across a variety of treatment factors (e.g., access to loan information, product features discussed, rates and terms offered, products discussed, questions asked, application documents discussed, actions inviting the potential customer to apply, assistance and creativity at application, courtesy, and customer service).

4
FAIR LENDING TESTING, 1991–2009

4.1 THE FORMS OF DISCRIMINATION

Lending discrimination may take the form of disparate (differential) treatment or disparate impact. Each may require different remedies and different techniques to detect and therefore different implications when setting public policy and lender guidelines to ensure sound sales and service practices and equal access to credit for minorities and non-minorities and other groups of consumers (female, male, young, and old).

Disparate treatment occurs when equally qualified individuals are treated differently due to their race or ethnicity, gender or age. In consumer credit, this may manifest itself in discouraging or providing different information to a potential Black applicant than to a similarly situated White applicant, or rejecting a Hispanic or Latino and accepting the similarly situated White applicant, or providing different and unfavorable terms to a Black female applicant from those offered to a similarly situated White female applicant.

Differential or disparate treatment may be classified as overt or subtle. Overt differences are those actions which are evident to the prospective borrower. Examples include a prospective borrower told to "go to another lender," or told that he or she "will *not* qualify" for the loan. Subtle differences are actions which are not noticeable to the borrower but nevertheless affect the prospective borrower's access to credit and ability to make an appropriate decision about credit. Examples include telling the Black potential borrower approval time will take 60 days while the similarly situated White potential borrower is told 30 days;

taking longer to approve the Black loan applicant than the potential White applicant; or making available to the potential Hispanic borrower only loans offering lower monthly payments but higher variable interest, while offering the potential White borrower a variety of loans including fixed rate and adjustable loans.

Disparate impact is when lender policies or actions are applied equally to minority and non-minority (or protected and non-protected) loan applicants but adversely impact Blacks, Hispanics, and other protected classes. If these policies do not have a business necessity they may be deemed discriminatory. For example, setting minimum loan amounts or minimum down payment requirements may adversely impact minorities more so than Whites. Minorities traditionally have lower household incomes and family wealth and therefore can only afford less costly homes and offer lower down payments to purchase a home. These policies may be deemed discriminatory unless they serve a business necessity or cannot be replaced by policies serving the same business purpose.

For public policy this means going further than ensuring equal treatment of minorities and non-minorities. It means that lender's business policies should be reviewed to identify and modify policies that have a disproportionately negative effect on minorities.

4.2 FAIR LENDING TESTING, FINDINGS, TRENDS, AND BEST PRACTICES

4.2.1 The Early to Mid-1990s

Market research and self-testing programs in the early to mid-1990s were used primarily to detect and help defend against allegations of discrimination. The programs emphasized the pre-application phase of the loan process and the extent to which pre-screening and discouragement occurred. To a lesser extent lenders made use of post-application surveys to assess the application phase and whether or not coaching and quality of assistance was similar for protected and non-protected classes.

The prospective loan customer in the early to mid-1990s encountered more restrictive loan underwriting guidelines than in the late 1990s and from 2000 to 2007. Most consumers applied for a loan in person. Call centers and telephone applications were just gaining in popularity. The industry and regulators were focused primarily on mortgage loans. Lenders approved customers and the secondary market encouraged financing of mortgage loans based on the cash flow of the consumer.

Housing expense represented no more than 28% of household income and total housing and debt obligations could not exceed 36% of income. In 2008 and 2009, due to restrictive credit markets, many lenders have returned to these housing and debt obligation ratios when evaluating credit worthiness.

During this time self-testing principally centered on the pre-application stage of the mortgage and home equity loan process. Of particular concern was whether or not lenders were pre-screening minorities and discouraging protected classes from applying. In this regard self-testing was used to measure differences in treatment between protected and non-protected classes and whether the differences were overt and subtle in nature. Overt differences are those actions which are evident to the prospective borrower. Examples include a prospective borrower told to "go to another lender," or told that he or she "will not qualify" for the loan. Subtle differences are those actions which are not noticeable to the borrower but nevertheless affect the prospective borrower's ability to make an appropriate decision about credit.

The typical mortgage testing scenario and experience encountered by non-minority or White testers and minority testers in the early to mid-1990s is described below.

> We decided to purchase our first home, so we visited a couple of local banks and a mortgage company. We told the representatives we just started to look for a home. They asked us about the purchase price of the home, whether we were renting now, and told us we needed to put down at least 10% of the purchase price. One bank said 20%. The representatives also asked us about our income and our auto and credit card payments, how much we had in checking and savings and whether or not we were employed and how much money we make. We answered the representatives and most said based on the information it looks like we would probably qualify for a 30-year fixed rate loan. The representatives also asked us to apply and said when we are ready to bring in proof of income and provide checking and saving account numbers and the contract. The representatives told us about a 30-year fixed rate mortgage and told us the monthly payment and the estimated costs of the loan. The mortgage company mentioned an adjustable rate mortgage in addition to a fixed rate mortgage. All the representatives said it would probably take 30 days to find out whether or not we were approved for the loan.[1]

4.2.1.1 The Objective of Pre-Application and Matched Pair Testing

During this time market research and self-testing undertaken by lenders with the encouragement of government regulators and enforcement agencies centered on the pre-application stage of the mortgage and home equity loan process. Of particular concern was whether or not lenders were pre-screening and discouraging protected classes from applying. Mystery shopping and matched pair testing were used to measure differences in treatment between protected and non-protected classes and whether the differences were overt and subtle in nature.

The power of the matched pair test is the side by side comparison of the experience encountered by the minority and non-minority testers.

> When first-time homebuyers begin shopping for a house, they need to learn about mortgages for which they can qualify and about house prices they can afford. This information can be provided by a variety of different sources, including mortgage lending institutions, real estate agents, and mortgage brokers. But if potential homebuyers cannot obtain full and fair access to information about mortgage financing, they may give up on their pursuit of homeownership, their housing search may be restricted, or they may be unable to negotiate the most favorable loan terms. Thus, pre-application inquiries about mortgage financing options represent a critical phase in the home buying process.[2]

Figure 4.1 describes how typical results from a matched pair testing study designed to detect disparate treatment are summarized. In addition to reporting differences by non-minority versus minority, most programs report differences by each race and ethnic group tested; for example, African American versus non-minority, Hispanic versus non-minority, and Asian American versus non-minority. The chart reveals that during non-minority tests representatives provided more information about annual percentage rate, appraisal fees, application fees, closing costs, monthly payment and available terms than they did during minority tests. This suggests that potential minority loan applicants may not be receiving all the information needed to make appropriate loan decisions.

Figure 4.2 summarizes the differences in treatment encountered by non-minority and minority matched pair testers during the period from 1991 to 1995 reported in a Fair Lending Progress Report by Barry Leeds & Associates and the author in November 1998.[3]

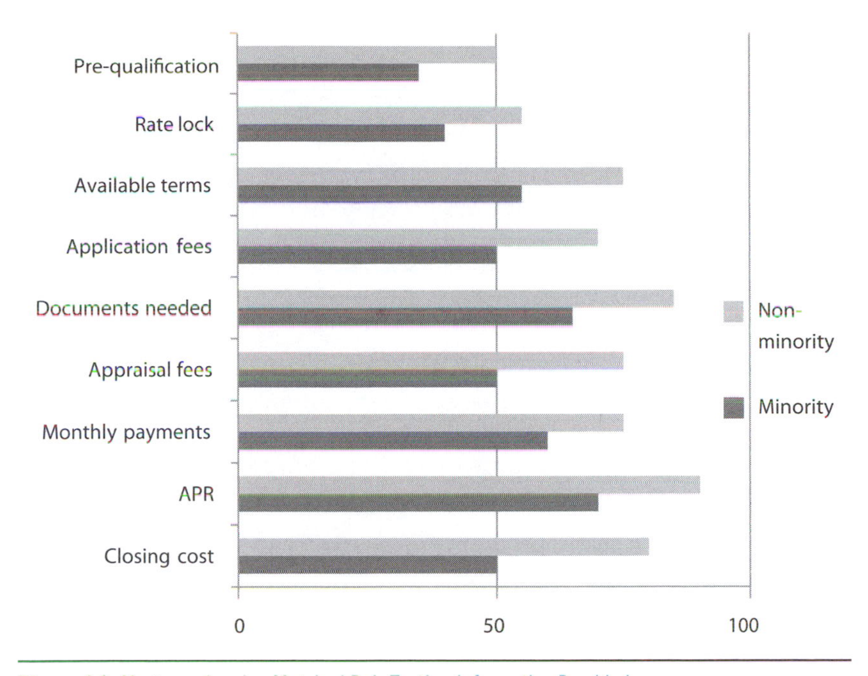

Figure 4.1 Mortgage Inquiry, Matched Pair Testing Information Provided

The most common differences noted above were typically drawn from bank retail offices with regard to mortgage and home equity/home improvement loans. These differences mostly involved African American versus non-minority tests, though at times less favorable treatment was noted for Hispanics.

The findings reflect instances where minorities are discouraged by representatives who inform them they probably would not qualify even though similarly situated White testers were told they would qualify. In addition, there were cases where representatives were more helpful to White testers by more often offering to pre-qualify them, informing White testers how to look better on the application, mentioning more products to White testers, and quoting a shorter approval time to White testers. In some instances, even though a financial institution emphasized building market share in the Hispanic community, the experience Hispanics encountered at a branch was far different from what was communicated in its advertising and outreach efforts. Hispanic testers waited more often and longer than White testers. Hispanic testers were less likely to be informed about loan terms and less likely to be offered an application and assistance to complete the application. In this case the financial institution failed to offer fair lending training and cultural

Summary of Findings: Instances of Disparate Treatment 1991–1995

Action	Type of Difference – Subtle or Overt
Discussed a wider variety of loans with non-minorities	Subtle
Mentioned more mortgage characteristics to non-minorities	Subtle
Follow-up phone calls made to non-minorities	Subtle
Minorities were quoted a longer approval time	Subtle
Minorities were less likely to be pre-qualified	Subtle
Minorities were less likely to be offered applications	Subtle
Minorities were quoted higher fees/interest rates	Subtle
Minorities were more likely to be told they wouldn't qualify or qualify for a lesser amount	Overt
Minorities were not told how they could "look better" on their application and non-minorities were told	Subtle
Minorities were less satisfied	Subtle
Minority testers waited longer	Subtle
Minority testers reported the transaction was rushed	Subtle

Figure 4.2 Summary of Findings: Instances of Disparate Treatment 1991–1995

sensitivity training to its branch staff. It thought that merely marketing to the Hispanic community would be enough to attract customers, build market share, and demonstrate that it was not redlining and restricting credit offers to Hispanic and minority communities.

4.2.1.2 The Philadelphia Commission on Human Rights Pre-Application Testing Program

In the early to mid-1990s the Philadelphia Commission on Human Rights with the support of a U.S. Housing and Urban Development (HUD) grant, in recognition that HMDA does not require lenders to keep records of loan inquiries, conducted a pre-application mortgage lending testing program.[4]

The goals of the program were: (1) to determine whether Black testers were treated differently from White testers when inquiring about a mortgage loan; (2) assess whether lenders discriminated based on neighborhood; (3) initiate complaints to HUD if violations occurred; and (4) require lenders to take steps to promote fair lending policies.

In total 192 matched tests were conducted at 68 lenders and 11 of the tests resulted in complaints to HUD. Two of the complaints involved terms and conditions at banks, one large and one small. The Black testers allegedly were treated differently from White testers with regard to services and treatment. It was determined that the Black testers were given less information on loan products and treated less courteously than White testers. The large bank agreed as a result of the testing to institute fair lending training. Another three complaints involved lender policies requiring 20% down. It was alleged that this policy has an adverse impact on minorities since there is a greater percentage of minorities than Whites who cannot afford a 20% down payment on a property in Philadelphia. One of the lenders agreed to change its underwriting criteria to allow consumers to put down 5% on the purchase of a home. The lender also agreed to advertise the change and to arrange to have all loan officers participate in fair lending training.

4.2.2 The Mid- to Late 1990s

The mid- to late 1990s saw increased emphasis on fair lending and self-testing by government regulators, enforcement agencies, and lenders. While the main emphasis was still on mortgage loans, attention turned toward home equity and home improvement as well as small business loans.

The latter part of the 1990s also saw the emergence of sub-prime lending and expanded and more flexible underwriting. In parallel, alternative delivery channels emerged as did automated underwriting, risk based pricing, and the use of credit scores in the approval and pricing of a loan. Lenders relied more on statistical analysis to assess the role of race in the approval decision and to help identify minority loan files to review for disparate treatment.

The experience of White mortgage loan testers and minority mortgage loan testers in the mid- to late 1990s now varied based on the type of lender, its policies, and the particular loan officer.

> *Sub-prime lender:* I called and asked for information about a mortgage loan. The representative introduced himself and the company and asked for my name and why I wanted the loan. I told him it was to buy a house. He congratulated me and said it was an important step. He then asked for the purchase price of the home and then for my social security number. I said I just needed to get information so I could decide if I wanted to apply. He said that without my social security number he could not provide me with information.

> *Bank:* I walked in the office and asked for information about a loan. The representative took my name and telephone number and also gave me the telephone number of the mortgage loan officer. I arranged a time to visit the branch and meet the loan officer. The representative asked me why I wanted a loan. I said it was to buy a house. The representative then asked for the purchase price and how much of a down payment I had. He went on to ask how much I had in my checking and savings accounts, our household income, and whether there were any other sources of income and cash for a down payment. He then mentioned several products, a fixed rate 30-year mortgage loan, an adjustable rate mortgage loan, and something he called a first time homebuyers loan.

> *Mortgage Company:* I called the mortgage company and asked if I could come by and meet with someone about a mortgage loan. The representative asked if I had a sales contract. I said no, I just started looking. The mortgage loan officer said he was busy and when I had a sales contract to call. I said I had a house in mind I wanted to make an offer but I needed information and really wanted to meet in person. He scheduled an appointment. When

> we met he asked me the purchase price and the amount of the loan. He also asked if I was currently renting and if this was the first time I was buying a home. He went on to ask how much money I had in savings and checking accounts, how much I had for a down payment, whether we were employed, and how much we made. He also asked about my debt. He then mentioned the types of loans available including a fixed rate loan for 30 and 25 years, an adjustable rate loan, balloon loan, and FHA. He recommended the 30-year fixed rate loan and went on to say that I could also apply for a home equity loan at the same time and that I could use the money from the home equity loan toward my down payment and to pay other expenses. He also mentioned a rate lock feature where I could lock in the rate for 30 or 60 days.

Pre-application testing still covered the same topics as those covered in the early 1990s. Although now whether or not lenders asked for the social security number and if they refused to provide information without a social security number was measured. In addition the pre-application mystery shops measured whether the lender attempted to pre-approve the tester. The programs also measured the mention of a broader list of loans including adjustable rate loans, balloon mortgages, first time homebuyer and FHA loans. Fees and pricing quoted to the testers were also more of a concern as was the offer to buy down the rate and pre-payment penalties.

4.2.2.1 Small Business Loan Matched Pair Testing

A small business owner's access to credit is fundamental to successful business operations, employment and household income, economic growth, and accumulation of wealth. Discrimination toward potential and current minority small business owners during the small business loan process may discourage minority small business creation and limit minority small business opportunities for revenue growth.

Significant gaps exist in small business ownership between Whites, Blacks, and Hispanics and between men and women. Blacks currently represent about 13% of the U.S. population but only own 5% of the businesses. Hispanics also account for roughly 13% of the population but only own about 7% of the small businesses. Women account for roughly half the population but only own about 30% of the small businesses (see Figure 4.3).

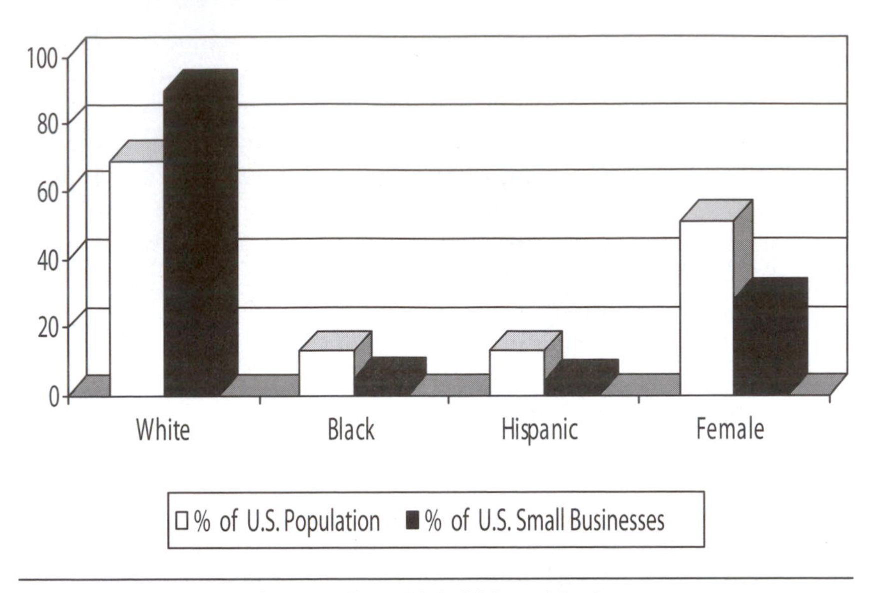

Figure 4.3 Small Business Owners by Race, Ethnic Origin, and Gender

It could be argued that perhaps there are other factors which lead to these disparities. However, NERA Economic Consulting conducted research using data from the Federal Reserve Board and the Survey of Small Business Finances. The research controlled for balance sheet and credit history and found when minority small business owners do apply for credit they are more likely to be denied and when they are approved minorities pay a higher interest rate than similar firms owned by non-minorities.[5]

In response to regulator concern and to be pro-active, many banks started to test the small business loan pre-application process to ensure compliance with the Equal Credit Opportunity Act. The small business pre-application testing programs use traditional matched pair testing and emphasize the detection of disparate treatment based on race and ethnic origin and gender.

A typical small business scenario and profile used in matched pair testing involves a sole proprietor operating a business from the home that is seeking to expand and move into an office. Loan amounts requested typically range from $50,000 to $100,000. The testers are armed with a profile describing the business. The profile covers:

- Loan purpose and nature of the business
- Number of employees and years in business

- Firm and small business owner financials
- Debt

Similar to mortgage and other types of matched pair tests and mystery shops the small business testers monitor access to the lender and small business loan information, products made available, invitation to apply, suitability or determining the needs of the customer, and customer rapport.

4.2.2.2 Post-Application Surveys

In the mid- to late 1990s, lenders increasingly made use of post-application surveys to ensure that the quality of assistance was of a nature that similarly maximized the opportunity for loan approval for minorities and non-minorities.

Figure 4.4 describes how post-application self-testing results are typically summarized. Results are disguised but reflect actual results. The chart depicts a situation where recent non-minority mortgage loan applicants are more likely to report a higher level of assistance than recent minority loan applicants. Non-minorities are more likely to report being offered a loan recommendation, receiving help when

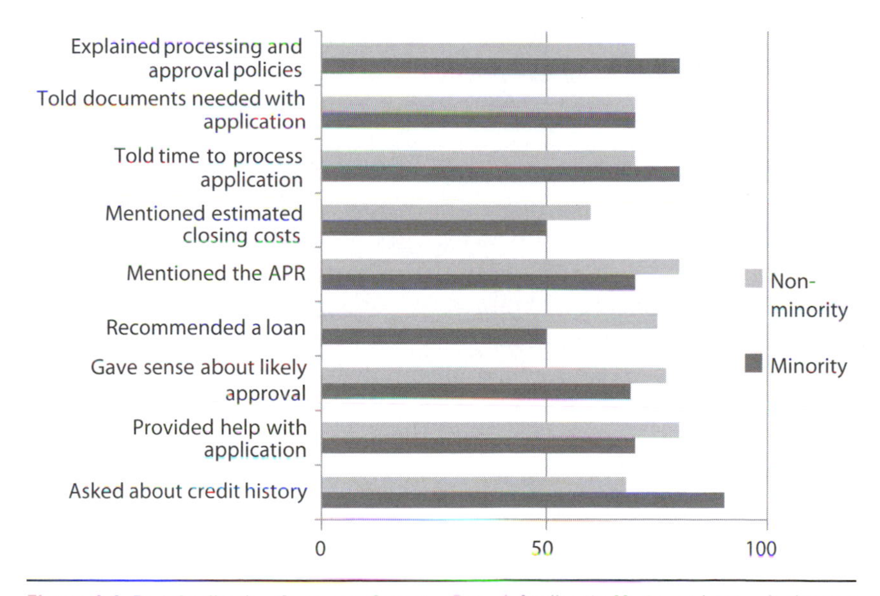

Figure 4.4 Post-Application Consumer Survey—Recent Applicants Mortgage Loan—Assistance at Application

completing the application, given a sense about likely approval, and quoted annual percentage rate and estimated closing costs. At the same time minorities are more likely to report they were asked about credit history, and that loan processing and approval policies were explained.

4.2.2.3 The Most Common Self-Testing Findings Mid- to Late 1990s

The mid- to late 1990s saw a heightened awareness of fair lending among financial institutions. This was primarily due to the emphasis placed on fair lending by regulatory and enforcement agencies. Regulator and enforcement agency attention to fair lending resulted in fewer Regulation B violations (e.g., informing testers they probably would not qualify) and fewer instances of disparate treatment uncovered by self-testing. In addition, lenders increasingly took the position that before an opinion about likely qualification could be provided to a potential customer, an application must be taken. This helped to ensure consistency in treatment during the pre-application loan process since it limited discretion on the part of mortgage loan representatives. When differences in treatment were encountered the differences entailed a more careful approach toward minorities. This approach generally resulted in quoting a longer approval time to minorities, steering minorities to FHA loans, asking more questions of minorities, informing minorities more about documents and information required with the application, and less often attempting to pre-approve loans for minorities.[6]

The above findings are drawn mainly from self-testing programs and post-application telephone surveys conducted for banks, bank owned mortgage companies, mortgage companies, and a smaller set of subprime lenders. The pre-application tests comprised in-person tests at branches and mortgage offices as well as telephone tests of call centers originating mortgages and home equity loans. Post-application surveys for the most part covered mortgage and home equity customers. The pre-application tests and post-application surveys comprised Whites, African Americans, and Hispanics (see Figure 4.5).

The most common differences were encountered during in-person testing at retail offices of banks where representatives sold more than one product. Representatives who sell more than one product—for example, checking and savings deposit products plus home equity loans and mortgage loans—typically are less knowledgeable about the more complex credit products. This tended to result in differences in the experiences encountered by minority and non-minority testers. These differences usually favored the non-minority testers. The most common

THE MOST COMMON SELF-TESTING FINDINGS MID- TO LATE 1990'S

Pre-application testing	Post-application surveys
• Heightened awareness of fair lending and treatment of minorities • Overall less differences favoring non-minorities • Favored treatment of minorities • Fewer Regulation B violations ("you probably won't qualify") • Less disparate treatment • Lender less likely to give opinion about qualification (no differences) • Some isolated instances (differences) – approval time (higher for minorities) – product steering (minorities to FHA) – more questions of minorities (assistance not skepticism) – non-minorities told about lock in feature and discounted rate if customer – less opinions about qualification to minorities – more documents required with application mentioned to minorities – less often attempt to pre-approve minorities	• Overall similar assistance provided • Some isolated instances (differences) – Minorities less likely to say the representative recommended a loan – Minorities less often told about pre-approval – Provide less assistance to minorities in completing the application – Less likely to ask minorities about other sources of income – Less likely to provide minorities with a sense of whether or not they would be approved

Figure 4.5 The Most Common Self-Testing Findings Mid- to Late 1990's

differences were typically less favorable for African Americans though there were instances where Hispanics received less favorable treatment. At times minorities received more favorable treatment probably owing to fair lending and diversity training instituted by the financial institution. Fewer differences were typically found with dedicated mortgage originators, particularly at bank owned mortgage companies, probably due to the level of product knowledge, product specialization, and emphasis on fair lending by regulated banks. The experience typically was generally of a much higher quality and very consistent.

4.2.2.4 Urban Institute Matched Pair Testing Study

In the late 1990s the U.S. Department of Housing and Urban Development contracted with the Urban Institute to conduct a pilot matched pair testing program in Los Angeles and Chicago. The purpose was to assess the effectiveness of paired testing for determining whether minorities receive the same assistance as Whites in the pre-application of the mortgage loan process.

The pilot test results show that in both Los Angeles and Chicago, African American and Hispanic homebuyers face a significant risk of receiving less favorable treatment than comparable Whites when they visit mortgage lending institutions to inquire about financing options. However in the majority of cases, minorities and Whites received equal treatment, or when differences occurred, they were equally likely to favor the minority as the White. But in both metropolitan areas, paired testing reveals statistically significant patterns of unequal treatment that systematically favor Whites.[7]

The study goes on to say unequal treatment takes different forms in the two metropolitan areas and for the two minority groups.

In Los Angeles:

- Blacks were offered less coaching than comparable White homebuyers, and were more likely to be encouraged to consider an FHA loan.
- Hispanics were denied basic information about loan amount and house price, told about fewer products, and received less follow-up compared to Anglo homebuyers.

In Chicago:

- Blacks were denied basic information about loan amount and house price, told about fewer products, offered less coaching, and received less follow-up than comparable White homebuyers.
- Hispanics were quoted lower loan amounts or house prices, told about fewer products, and offered less coaching than comparable Anglo homebuyers.

These patterns of unequal treatment occurred regardless of whether the two members of a tester pair met with the same loan officer or with different loan officers. Another example of differences found in the pilot Urban Institute study is shown below.

> Two female testers, one White and one Black, visited the same Los Angeles area lender two days apart and met with the same loan officer. The testers told the loan officer that they were first-time homebuyers and needed assistance in figuring out a home price range and a loan amount for which they might qualify. The loan officer requested and obtained detailed information on household income, debts, and assets from both testers and asked about their respective credit situations. He then estimated that the white tester would qualify for a $332,500 loan to purchase a $350,000 home and, but estimated that the black tester would qualify for a $237,500 loan to purchase a $245,000 home. The loan officer told the white tester that a seller would likely pay some of the closing costs, but no mention was made about seller assistance to the black tester. The loan officer also told the white tester that it was a good idea to have a home inspection conducted prior to purchase, while the loan officer did not mention anything about the value of a home inspection to the black tester. The loan officer provided a complete loan application package to the white tester, but not to the black tester.[8]

4.2.3 2000 to 2009

The nature of the credit marketplace and the experience consumers encountered when searching for credit changed dramatically in 2000. The rise of risk based pricing, credit scoring models, automated underwriting, and increased funding from the secondary markets brought with it an expanded credit marketplace in terms of lenders and a wider array of product offerings. Almost every credit market was affected, including mortgages and home equity, personal consumer and unsecured lines of credit, small business and credit card. Along with the expanded credit marketplace came the sale of ancillary credit products such as credit protection, unemployment insurance, etc. Many lenders also moved into complementary product lines to garner more fees (e.g. title insurance). Sub-prime lending grew dramatically along with expanded product sets, delivery and broker channels, sales forces, and sales and marketing programs aimed at attracting customers and with it fees.

Consumers faced a sharply increased number of product choices and lenders. These choices were present across different types of credit, including mortgages, refinance, home equity, credit cards, unsecured credit lines, auto, and personal loans. And the way lenders deliver products changed. Now the lender marketed its products through stores, telephone, Internet, mail, and third parties (e.g., mortgage brokers). In addition the approval process accelerated. Consumers applied and were approved for many products within days if not minutes. Gone were the days where the length of the process gave consumers the chance to search, acquire knowledge, and build comfort with the product.

Lenders adapted their training and sales scripts to fit the new environment of fast and flexible credit. Some sales scripts emphasized rapport building at the introductory stage of the customer lender relationship. Rapport building played a particularly important role in the sales process. Initial questions were asked about why the money was needed and if there were key life milestones such as a child going to college, a need to update the kitchen, or an upcoming wedding. The representatives were trained to congratulate the potential customer and position themselves as a financial advisor who could help them use credit and the equity in their home to help secure these milestones. Once the representatives established how credit could be used to achieve the goals for the potential loan applicant the representatives moved quickly to obtain the consumer's social security number in order to run a credit check, generate a credit score, and then fit the consumer into a product based on their credit score and profile. Little education was offered to the consumer. "What if" scenarios depicting monthly mortgage payments and potential savings over current loans were provided to consumers to show potential monthly savings and cash out dollar amounts. In many cases this was misleading insofar as the "what if" scenario did not accurately incorporate the terms of the current loan.

At the same time regulators and government enforcement agencies were not focused on fair lending, adherence to the Equal Credit Opportunity Act and Fair Housing Act, and unfair sales practices. Attention was on privacy, money laundering, and the Bank Secrecy Act.

Figure 4.6 displays the changes to the credit marketplace that occurred from the early 1990s through the turn of the century and continued until 2009. In each time period the first bar refers to the degree of flexible underwriting offered by lenders, the second bar pertains to products/channels used by financial institutions to market loans, the third bar refers to fast approval of loan applications, the fourth bar

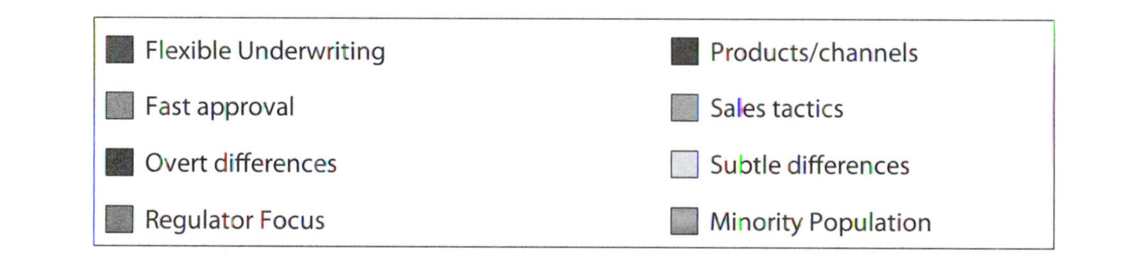

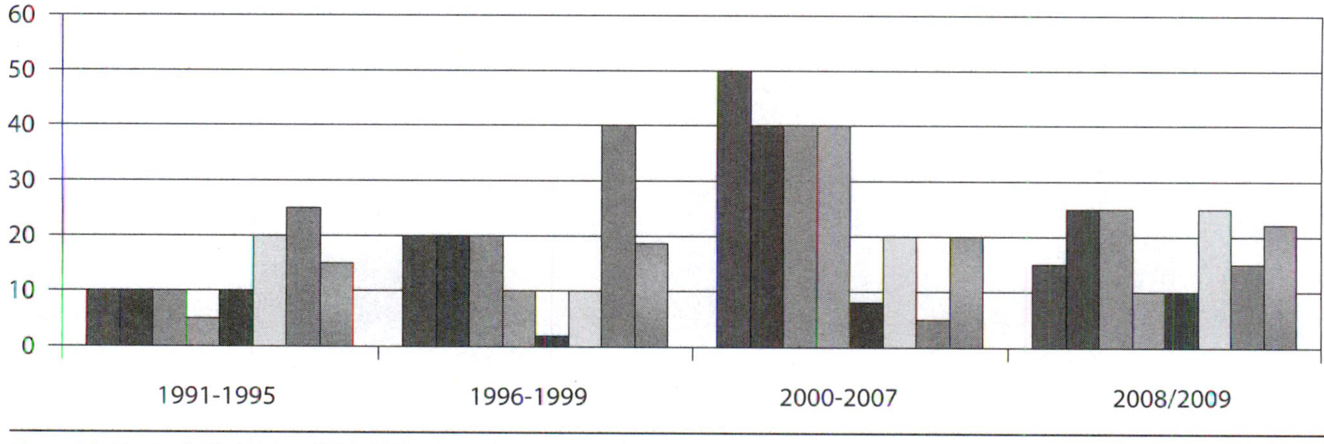

Figure 4.6 The Credit Marketplace 1991–2009, "Visual Depiction of Changes" based on Authors Opinion and Tests Completed

describes aggressive sales tactics undertaken by financial institutions, the fifth and sixth bars refer to overt and subtle differences in treatment, which did not favor minority testers versus non-minority testers, identified during matched pair and self-testing programs, the seventh bar describes the degree of regulator focus on fair lending, and the last or eighth bar pertains to the percent of the minority population in the United States.

Figure 4.6 depicts a sharp reduction in regulator focus on fair lending issues beginning in 2000 and lasting until early 2009. The decline in attention paid by regulators toward fair lending was associated with sharp increases in aggressive sales tactics by financial institutions and an uptick in overt and subtle differences identified during matched pair testing and self-testing.

These developments created an environment more prone to representatives engaging in unfair or deceptive acts or practices. This in turn increased the risk associated with customer dissatisfaction, harm to a company's reputation, and even litigation and government enforcement actions. Customers needed to be especially careful insofar as they ran the increased risk of applying for the wrong product and paying higher rates and fees.

In 2002 the Office of the Comptroller of the Currency issued an Advisory Letter describing the current marketing and sales environment as posing an increased risk of unfair sales practices. The Advisory Letter warned financial institutions that employees engaging in practices that harm customers can undermine the lender's reputation and its ability to retain customers.[9]

An example of unfair or deceptive acts during this time is the allegation against the Associates. The Associates was a large finance company offering personal unsecured loans, real estate, and home equity loans to consumers across the United States. The allegations involved representatives making false statements about the benefits of debt consolidation. The allegations included the Associates calling customers and describing how the consumer could save money each month through an Equity Advantage Plan, typically a home equity loan. Here the Associates representative would describe to the consumer a "What-if scenario" showing the purported monthly savings and benefits of consolidating short term, unsecured debt, and home loan debt in a new home equity loan, typically 15 to 20 years. This comparison assumed the same monthly savings over 15 to 20 years even though the short term debt was for 5 years. In addition, the what-if scenarios did not factor in real estate taxes and insurance, which consumers needed to pay out of pocket. Still another allegation involved packing or selling unwanted or needed products to consumers. Here the allegations included representatives telling consumers that payment protection was included in the monthly payment quote but did not describe the added cost of the payment protection. In many instances representatives included payment protection in the monthly payment quote without telling the customer payment protection was included.[10]

Citifinancial, the firm that acquired the Associates undertook a self-testing program which assessed its pre-application and application sales practice in the form of mystery shopping.[11] The purpose of the self-testing was to ensure its policies were being followed and to enhance customers' confidence in its practices.

In the sub-prime area market research and testing programs were conducted by lenders with sub-prime products and community groups. The National Community Reinvestment Coalition (NCRC), a community group, conducted a pre-application matched pair testing program of sub-prime lenders. The program consisted of 48 tests. Forty of the tests were in-person or site tests and 8 of the tests were conducted over the telephone. The tester contacted the lending institution and indicated that they (the tester and spouse) were interested in obtaining a home equity loan. All testers were given a profile indicating that they were qualified for a prime loan. All tester profiles indicated that the testers were married and were long time homeowners with substantial equity in their homes. All testers had a low loan to value ratio (below 80% after the requested home equity loan), a good debt to income ratio (below the 36% often used for conventional loans), and the tester represented that they had good credit. While tester profiles were substantially similar, African American testers were given profiles which made them slightly more qualified, in that they had more income, better ratios, higher credit score, and longer time in the home and on the job.

NCRC conducted subprime fair lending testing of large lenders in six major metropolitan areas throughout the United States. The tests covered 12 sub-prime lenders with retail outlets serving the metropolitan areas of Atlanta, Baltimore, Chicago, the District of Columbia, Los Angeles, and New York City. The tests were conducted with the assistance and cooperation of local NCRC members, community organizations, civil rights activists, and consumer protection organizations.

4.2.3.1 Results

NCRC reports the testing showed a 45% rate of disparate treatment based on race.

The types of differences in treatment reported by NCRC include:

> The White testers were more often "referred up" to the lender's prime lending division.
>
> The White testers were more often quoted interest rates.
>
> The White testers were quoted lower interest rates, or range of rates.
>
> The White testers were given more detailed information.
>
> The White testers were often assumed to be qualified, and given recommendations based upon assumed qualifications.
>
> The loan officers spent more time with the White testers.
>
> The White testers received more follow-up.
>
> The Black testers were often asked about the condition of their house; the White testers were not.
>
> The Black testers were more often asked what they wanted to do with the money.[12]

NCRC provided narratives on two of the tests:

> In Baltimore, testers met with the same loan officer at a branch of the sub-prime affiliate of a major national lender. The loan officer assumed the White tester was over-qualified and without asking any financial questions, told her she could get better rates at the prime branch of the parent company. The loan officer also gave the White tester general rate ranges. However, the loan officer would not give the Black tester any rate information, citing the need for a credit check. The loan officer crumpled and discarded the Black tester's application when she would not reveal her social security number.
>
> In another test in Baltimore at a suburban branch of a major sub-prime lender, the White tester was told of a 5.75%, 30-year fixed interest rate, while the Black tester was told the 30-year rate was 8.85%. The White tester was told the 2-year adjustable rate was 4.99% and the Black tester was told the rate for that product

> was 7.6%. The Black tester was told that since her husband made more money (just slightly more), the lender would rely on the husband's income and credit. The White female tester was not asked about income, nor told about this policy.[13]

4.2.3.2 Fair Housing Center of Greater Boston Matched Pair Testing

In another research study investigating the extent of discrimination in mortgage lending, the Fair Housing Center of Greater Boston conducted a matched pair testing exercise in October 2005 through January 2006. Black, Hispanic, Asian, Caribbean, and White volunteers were recruited and trained and asked to visit specific mortgage lenders and inquire about a mortgage loan. In all 20 matched pair tests were completed. The volunteers or testers were provided with matched profiles. Ten of the pairs were provided with good credit profiles, credit scores of about 750, while the other 10 pairs were provided with mediocre credit profiles, credit scores of about 650. The Black, Hispanic, Asian, and Caribbean tester was provided with a slightly better credit profile than the White tester. The Fair Housing Center reported differences favoring the White tester in 9 out of the 20 matched pair tests. Seven of the tests were large enough to form the basis of legal action.

Descriptions of the differences reported by the Fair Housing Center of Greater Boston are shown below.

> An African American tester with a good credit score of 670 visited a bank to inquire about a mortgage. She was told that the closing fee would be $8,000 to $9,000, although other tests in this investigation indicated that average closing fee was $2,000 to $3,000. The bank representative also told her that her credit score of 670 was below average; other tests indicated that a credit score of 670 was well above average. Finally, the bank representative told her that the bank usually dealt with commercial lending, and did not really provide residential mortgages. In contrast, the White tester with a credit score of 640 who visited the same bank was told by two different loan officers that the bank provided home mortgage loans, and was not told that her credit score was below average.

> An Asian American tester with credit score of 770 and a white tester with credit score of 740 visited a mortgage lending company. The Asian American tester received a referral to a realtor to help her find a home. The White tester was told about two

realtors who could provide her with discounts on fees as well as help her find a home. The White tester also received a $500 certificate toward closing fees; the Asian American tester received no certificate or offer of a discount.

A Latino tester with a credit score of 670 and a White tester with a credit score of 640 visited a mortgage lending company. The lender provided both with quotes on monthly payments, and the Latino loan seeker's quote was $254 per month more than the White loan seeker's quote for a 30-year fixed loan, and $140 per month more for a blended loan The lender also told the Latino loan seeker that she would need private mortgage insurance (PMI), which would cost $309 per month. The lender did not bring up PMI to the White loan seeker. The lender did tell the White loan seeker about how to get a better loan product when your credit score is under 680, but did not discuss this with the Latino loan seeker, whose score was also below 680. Finally, the White loan seeker was given informational literature about different loan products and loan processes, and received a follow-up e-mail from the lender. The Latino loan seeker did not receive any literature or follow-up e-mail.

An African American tester with a credit score of 770 and a White tester with a credit score of 740 inquired at a mortgage lending company. The lender gave the White homebuyer an explanation of six different types of mortgage loans, naming advantages and disadvantages of each. The White homebuyer asked about getting a blended loan to avoid PMI, and the lender replied that the second loan in the two-loan "blended loan" has high interest, so a blended loan is a bad idea. At the end of the meeting, the lender asked the White homebuyer for her address so that he could send a thank-you card. When the African American homebuyer visited, she was told about one loan product only: the blended loan. The lender did not mention the high interest on the second loan or any other loan products.

An African American tester with a credit score of 670 and a White tester with a credit score of 640 were sent to a bank without a prior appointment and inquired about mortgage products. The loan officer referred the African American tester to another loan specialist at a different branch without giving her any information about loan products. The African American tester had to make an appointment with the second officer and then meet with him to get information about loans. The White tester walked into the same initial branch and the same lender met with the White tester on the spot and discussed loan products, rather than referring her to a different branch. The lender told the White tester that borrowers receive a $2,000 credit toward the closing fee if the borrower has an account with the bank. While the loan officer encouraged the African American tester to open an account to receive a discount on closing, he did not tell the tester the size of the discount. Lastly, the lender sent a follow-up e-mail to the White tester explaining all the loan products this bank offered and their rates and estimated monthly payments. The African American tester was not asked for her e-mail address and received no follow-up information.

An African American tester with a credit score of 670 and a White tester with a credit score of 640 visited a mortgage lending company. The lender provided informational pamphlets about mortgages to the White tester, but not the African American tester.

An African American tester with a credit score of 770 and a White tester with a credit score of 740 visited a bank. Their visits to the lender were comparable, but after the visit, only the White tester received a follow-up e-mail with more information about different loan products and a $500 certificate toward the closing fee. The African American tester did not receive follow-up contact or the $500 offer.

An Asian American tester with a credit score of 770 and a White tester with a credit score of 740 inquired at a bank. The lender recommended a 30-year fixed loan with 0.75 points to the Asian American, quoting a monthly payment of $3,350, not including tax and insurance. To the White home seeker, the lender recommended a 5-year ARM with no points, with a monthly payment of $3,225, including tax and insurance. This means that the Asian American home seeker was quoted approximately $3,600 more for the closing fee because of the point and $125 plus tax and insurance per month more than her White counterpart. The lender told the White home seeker that an ARM was a better choice than a 30-year fixed rate because most people who buy homes in the town she was considering refinance within 5 years. The Asian American home seeker was looking to buy a home in the same town. The lender gave the White home seeker numerous information sheets, including brochures about different types of loans, an ARM loan procedure worksheet, 2006 property tax information, and a pre-approval guidebook. The lender did not give any information sheets to the Asian American. While it is impossible to know exactly what product would have been better for either home seeker, the lender characterized the ARM as a better choice by giving the White person an explanation and explanatory material while providing the person of color with neither to explain his recommendation for a fixed rate mortgage.

A Latino tester with a credit score of 670 and a White tester with a credit score of 640 inquired at a bank. Both were told about 30-year fixed and unspecified blended loans (that is, the lender did not tell either tester the specific terms of the blend), but the White home seeker was also told about an ARM loan. The White home seeker was encouraged to submit an application as soon as possible, while the lender did not talk with the Latino home seeker about an application. The White home seeker was given pamphlets about different mortgages, a guidebook about mortgages, a worksheet for the cost of the mortgage, and an application; the Latino home seeker received none of these materials.[14]

4.2.3.3 Discrimination by Mortgage Brokers in Wholesale Channels

From 2004 to 2006, the National Community Reinvestment Coalition (NCRC), conducted mystery shopping of mortgage brokers, both large and small.[15] NCRC's broker testing yielded a total of 106 complete, matched pair tests. Individuals located in the metropolitan areas of Atlanta, Baltimore, Chicago, the District of Columbia, Houston, Los Angeles, and St. Louis tested brokers that were local, established businesses. In conducting the broker testing, NCRC found several companies with particularly egregious initial results. In these cases, testers were again dispatched for follow-up testing to confirm and further investigate the practices of these companies.

Of the 106 total tests, 84 separate companies were tested, the difference being as a result of 22 follow-up tests. NCRC describes some of the results as follows:

1. African Americans and Latinos were discouraged 25% of the time concerning their efforts to meet with a broker, while comparison testers were discouraged only 12% of the time in their efforts to obtain credit.
2. Brokers spent more time with White shoppers than with African Americans and Latinos, spending on average 39 minutes with White testers and only 27 minutes with African American and Latino testers.
3. White mortgage seekers received greater encouragement over 60% of the time, while African Americans and Latinos were questioned about their credit over 32% of the time. White shoppers were only questioned about credit 13% of the time.
4. White mortgage seekers had specific products discussed with them 91% of the time, while African Americans and Latinos had specific products discussed with them 76% of the time. Further, White testers received two rate quotes for every one quoted to African American and Latino testers.
5. NCRC documented pricing discrimination in 25% of the fair lending tests, and noted that fees were discussed 62% of the time with White testers but only 35% of the time with "protected testers."
6. Fixed rate loans were discussed 77% of the time with White testers but only 50% of the time with African American and Latino testers.

The NCRC testing clearly shows the power of matched pair testing and in particular mystery shopping as a tool to identify the experience of potential loan customers. Mystery shopping clearly portrays the sales process and the ease or difficulty consumers face in obtaining credit information.

The ability of consumers to obtain information in the pre-application phase of the loan process became even more important with the proliferation of products to choose from. The ability to obtain information when searching for credit remains extremely important even when loan products are fewer and underwriting policies and flexibility rigid. Without information consumers are restricted in their ability to make appropriate credit decisions and may make decisions that cannot be easily corrected, especially in credit markets that are restricted and where general economic conditions are contracting. The use of market research by government and lenders not only helps to manage risk but can also ensure that consumers are receiving the information needed to make appropriate credit decisions.

4.2.3.4 Lender Self-Testing to Detect Discrimination

From 2000 to 2007 minority declination ratios decreased in conjunction with the growth of sub-prime lending and risk based pricing. The number of lenders using market research for self-testing also declined. In addition financial institutions were less likely to report regulators recommending mystery shopping and post-application testing surveys. Some pro-active lenders, owing to their prominence in the market, continued rigorous self-testing and undertook mystery shopping or post-application testing. Other lenders started to conduct more limited or targeted self-testing or mystery shopping programs. The more limited programs were termed "temperature" checks or evaluations. The approach is much smaller in scale and cannot be used to determine whether or not patterns or practices exist across the organization. Rather a smaller but more concentrated number of tests are conducted in selected major markets and delivery channels. For example a multi-state bank can examine its pre-application loan process in three to five major markets deemed "higher risk." In a self-test designed to measure adherence to the Equal Credit Opportunity Act and Fair Housing Act, a financial institution can select major markets and markets with a high proportion of protected classes. Testing is conducted in these markets under the premise that if a problem or major area of risk exists the issue will manifest itself in these markets. The learning gained from the tests in these markets is applied to other markets. Such an approach is limited in the sense that the results are specific to only those locations tested and the findings may be discounted by management due to the limited number of tests that are completed. In effect, even if issues are uncovered the financial institution may not act due to the limited number of tests and questions about the reliability of the findings. The temperature check approach is also subject to accusations that the lender is really not interested in finding and resolving possible fair lending issues, but is only interested in showing regulators and enforcement agencies that self-testing is being conducted.

Still another approach is to target markets and products where HMDA data, account growth, withdrawn application, and statistical modeling indicate a greater source of risk; for example, substantially higher minority denial rates, disproportionately fewer minority loan applications, higher minority application withdrawal rates, or a disproportionate number of minorities and older customers carrying credit insurance. Such an approach seeks to determine whether the cause is due to disparate treatment or misleading sales practices.

Lenders also became concerned with wholesale and indirect lending channels as they recognized the risk and liability associated with funding third party loans. Mystery shopping or self-testing programs were undertaken to test mortgage brokers on a matched pair and monadic basis. Mortgage brokers are selected for testing based on size of business, complaints, file reviews, and regression models. The tests even specify the protected classes, African American, Hispanic, Asian, gender and age of the testers, and the product scenario to be tested. Tests are conducted on-site and via the telephone. At times matched pair, triad, and monadic or one-off tests were conducted. Post-application consumer surveys were used both in terms of mortgage brokers and indirect auto. The surveys were conducted with recently closed mortgage and auto loan customers. The interview covers the entire loan process, pre-application or sales, application and underwriting, and closing. The survey determines if customers are satisfied with and understand the product purchased. It measures the customer's knowledge of the terms and conditions of the loan, whether or not the terms and conditions met the customer's expectation and any ancillary products sold and if these products were properly explained to the customer.

Figure 4.7 shows instances of disparate treatment and unfair sales practices based on self-testing programs conducted from 2000 through 2008.[16]

At times differences were found when consumers were asked for a social security number during the early stages of the pre-application sales process. This was noted for the most part at finance company, mortgage company, and sub-prime lenders. The policy of asking for the potential customer's social security number early in the sales process seemed to result in the minority receiving far less and sometimes no information. This was true for African Americans and Hispanics. When differences were noted concerning information provided to testers they occurred for the most part during in-person tests with branch employees at retail banks, mortgage companies (both bank owned and independent), and finance companies. There were also more problematic markets due to differences in treatment between minorities and non-minorities. These markets are for the most part consistent across lenders. There were also some individual cases at retail banks, especially during home equity and to some extent mortgage pre-application testing, where more favorable treatment of minorities was found. In these cases the financial institutions were conducting fair lending and diversity training and efforts were underway to develop business in minority and especially Hispanic communities.

When post-application survey results reported a greater willingness to help, recommend a loan, and offer an opinion about likely

INSTANCES OF DISPARATE TREATMENT AND OTHER ISSUES 2000–2008

Pre-application Testing	Post application Testing
• Little or no overt differences 2000–2007 • More overt differences in 2008 – Do not qualify – Qualify for lower loan amount – Qualify for lower home value – Require higher down payment • More subtle differences in 2008 – Different information – Different questioning – Different products discussed • More favorable treatment of minorities 2000-2007 – Emphasizing market share in emerging customer segments – Increased sensitivity to minorities • The use of credit scoring in the sales process at times resulting in differential treatment favoring non-minorities 2000–2007 • Less and more inconsistent use of credit scoring in 2008 to screen potential applicants	• At times a greater willingness to help non-minorities • Non-minorities more likely to say the loan officer offered a positive opinion on likely approval • Older customers report receiving less information and help than younger customers 2000–2007 • Some confusion about the nature and requirement of credit insurance between minorities and non-minorities 2000–2007 • Less lenders offering credit insurance in 2008 • Confusion as to the role of the mortgage broker and their relationship to the lender for both minorities and non-minorities • At times minorities more likely to say "delays cost us money" • Minorities less likely to say the loan process is prompt • Minorities more likely to report being contacted by the lender to ascertain interest in the lender's products 2000–2007

- Advice against escrow to lower monthly payment
- Offering Interest Only and Option ARM to lower monthly payment without describing lack of principal payment and fully indexed rate and maximum monthly payment
- Gender differences some favoring males, Hispanic female vs. Hispanic male, African American female vs. African American male, etc
- Insufficient staffing to handle Spanish calls 2000–2007
- At times insufficient staffing to handle all calls in 2008
- Telephone based service differences at times favoring non-minorities
- Differences in:
  - Approval time quoted, longer for minorities and females
  - Closing costs quoted, inconsistent
- Poor or no explanation of points and APR to minorities and females
- Problematic markets
- Inconsistency in small business loan information based on dedicated loan officers versus bankers 2000–2007
- Minorities more likely to say the lender did not return my calls
- Non-minorities more likely to report the loan officer offered a recommendation
- Small but substantial proportion of customers not aware of APR being discussed during sales process

Figure 4.7 Instances of Disparate Treatment and Other Issues 2000–2008

qualification among White loan applicants, they were generally encountered at mortgage and bank owned mortgage companies, finance companies, and sub-prime lenders. Comments that "delays cost us money" were mentioned in a small percentage of surveys with loan applicants. When issues regarding credit insurance were detected it reflected a small but meaningful percentage of minority and non-minority loan customers who indicated confusion about the product and whether or not it was required to obtain the loan. The implication was that a small but meaningful number of loan customers were under the impression credit insurance was required. This occurred at finance companies and sub-prime companies because these lenders offered the product. Post-application surveys were also able to detect loan flipping or encouraging customers to refinance. Minorities were more likely than Whites to report lenders, primarily sub-prime and finance companies, contacting them about refinancing. The surveys also surfaced instances where Whites more often than minorities were told they would probably qualify for the loan by mortgage representatives. This occurred more often than not at mortgage companies and banks.

Starting in 2008 and coincidental with more restrictive underwriting, self-testing uncovered more subtle differences in the treatment of minorities and non-minorities. Testers were also more likely to be told they would not qualify, qualify for a lower loan amount than requested, or qualify but with a higher down payment.

It should be noted that the instances of disparate treatment and other issues noted above for "2000–2008," "mid 1990s–late 1990s," and "1991–1995" were found during self-testing programs voluntarily undertaken by lenders. As such it may be argued that the results underestimate the extent of these issues among all lenders. The results portrayed represent a variety of financial institutions, including mid-size and large retail banks, bank owned mortgage companies, finance companies, sub-prime lenders, and tests among mortgage brokers. Many of these programs are conducted with lenders that have substantial branch networks and a number of employees, which makes the management of sales and service practices extremely difficult. Often the self-testing programs were undertaken due to complaints, investigations, and others undertaken as part of a fair lending program. Hence the findings are drawn from a mix of lenders, some of which have problems or have reason to believe there are problems and sought to identify problems, the extent of the problems, and take remedial actions to resolve the problems. Other lenders undertook self-testing prior to a fair lending exam. Many of the findings are drawn from programs that are ongoing and conducted every year or every other year. In addition some of the most common issues and instances of disparate treatment were found at the lenders who conduct testing over time and are probably a direct reflection of the changes in the industry, and management and employee turnover. For example, the introduction of credit scoring, risk based pricing, and desktop underwriting at times resulted in consumers and protected classes receiving less information in the loan process because representatives would often proclaim the need for a credit report before providing loan information.

5

MEASURING FAIR TREATMENT OF CONSUMERS IN THE CREDIT CARD AND DEBIT CARD MARKETPLACE

Market research can monitor and help detect and resolve problems in other financial product sectors critical to consumers' day-to-day quality of life. Products such as credit cards, debit cards, and investments are crucial. Time tested market research methodologies can help ensure consumers are receiving appropriate and understandable information in order to make appropriate decisions about financial products and the goods they purchase. This benefits consumers, financial institutions, and the nation. The consumer benefits in terms of being offered products that meet their needs and information needed to make appropriate decisions. The ability to better understand the features and benefits of financial products not only helps the consumer make better decisions about how to use financial products, but also helps her or him to make better decisions about the goods purchased. The financial institution benefits in terms of better meeting consumer needs and building long lasting and profitable relationships. The nation benefits in terms of a more efficient marketplace.

Credit cards and debit cards play an integral role in day-to-day consumer transactions. The cards facilitate the purchase of goods and services and enable consumers to make purchases and pay for the purchases over time. Many purchases are dependent on the use of either a credit card or debit card: a hotel or airline ticket reservation and purchase, an Internet purchase, and dining out are just some examples. The increased velocity of transactions and number of purchases facilitated by credit cards and debit cards fosters long term economic growth assuming consumers make appropriate decisions about whether or not to use the cards.

In 2008 78% of households in the United States had a credit card[1] and it is estimated that almost 13.9% of consumer disposable income went to pay credit card debt.[2] According to the Government Accounting Office's (GAO) November 2009 report on credit cards and interchange fees, the use of credit cards has grown dramatically both in terms of dollar volume and transactions. The GAO reports that in 2007 credit card transaction volume exceeded $1.9 trillion versus slightly more than $600 billion in 1991, while the number of transactions grew from slightly more than 6 billion in 1991 to almost 30 billion in 2007.[3] It is estimated by the American Bankers Association that more than half of the retail transactions in the United States are made through the use of cards, either credit cards or debit cards.[4]

The consumer's ability to understand the terms and features of credit cards and debit cards helps foster more informed decisions about purchases and when to use these products. Given the integral role credit cards and debit cards play in consumer purchases and the payment system it is important that consumers make appropriate decisions about the use of credit and debit cards. Market research can assess consumer needs and consumer understanding or misunderstanding of the terms and conditions of these products. The information can help guide public policy and regulations to help ensure that consumers are provided with the information needed to make appropriate decisions. In addition, market research can monitor consumer satisfaction with credit cards and debit cards and the treatment consumers receive when applying for and using credit and debit cards to ensure consumer needs are being met fairly and based on sound financial practices.

5.1 DEBIT CARDS

The fees applied that are associated with the use of debit cards present an example of the need for consumers to clearly understand the terms and features of the financial products used to conduct everyday transactions. Research conducted by the Center for Responsible Lending point out that almost one out of three consumers is enrolled in overdraft protection and the average overdraft fee is $34 for typically a $20 purchase. Consumers who earn less than $50,000 per year are more likely to be enrolled in this fee based overdraft protection while consumers who earn more are more likely to be enrolled in a line of credit linked to their checking accounts. A consumer telephone survey among 2,000 checking account customers across the United States completed by the Center for Responsible Lending in January 2008 revealed that almost 9 out of 10 consumers believe they should be given the option of including overdraft protection with their checking account even though most banks automatically included the service at the time and most consumers, slightly more than 7 out of 10, wanted their debit card purchases declined if they would result in a fee.[5]

Based on the increased use of debit cards and financial institutions' policy of charging overdraft fees, the Federal Reserve sought to develop new rules governing disclosures about the service. As part of the review the Federal Reserve conducted consumer testing. The consumer testing consisted of a series of in-depth consumer interviews that assessed consumer awareness of overdraft protection and charges; preferences regarding the service and the efficacy of disclosures in communicating the choices consumers have in obtaining overdraft protection; the potential fees involved in overdrafts; and how overdrafts are handled by the financial institution. The research conducted by the Federal Reserve Board shows that many consumers were not aware they were enrolled in overdraft protection and could incur overdrafts and thought transactions would be declined if they had insufficient funds. In addition a majority of the consumers interviewed said they would prefer not to be enrolled unless they affirmatively consented or opted in.[6]

5.2 CREDIT CARDS

5.2.1 The Credit Card Responsibility and Disclosure Act

In May 2009 the Credit Card Responsibility and Disclosure Act sought to remedy several credit card practices which were considered by many to be unfair and detrimental to the consumer. Among the remedies were enhanced disclosure requirements and transparency of credit card terms and conditions. Among the more important are requirements to inform consumers about the time period to pay off their credit card debt, the interest paid and total cost to the consumer if minimum payments are made, the monthly payment required to pay off the balance in full in 36 months, and a toll free number the consumer can call for credit counseling. These disclosures are to be made in a table that provides a clear and concise description of these disclosures. The act also requires a credit issuer to consider the consumer's ability to make the required payments under the terms of the credit card account. Arbitrary rate increases based on universal default are prohibited, as well as fees for paying credit card debt by telephone, mail, or electronic transfer, late fees when the credit issuer delays credit of payment, and double cycle billing or paying interest on the average balances over the last two billing periods were also eliminated.

Many of the changes implemented in the Credit Card Responsibility and Disclosure Act were based on the Federal Reserve Board's review of Regulation Z, which implements the Truth and Lending Act, which began in 2004. The act requires that certain information about costs and terms be disclosed in order to facilitate the informed use of credit by consumers. This includes the annual percentage rate; fees associated with credit availability and account activity or inactivity; minimum finance charge and transaction charges; grace period; balance computation method; a statement that the charges incurred due to use of the charge card are due upon receipt of the periodic statement; and the fees associated with a cash advance, late payment, exceeding the credit limit, and a balance transfer. These disclosures are made on the application or direct mail solicitation and are made orally during telephone applications or solicitations initiated by the card issuer. The regulation requires these disclosures to be in a prominent location and in the form of a table.[7]

The Federal Reserve Board's review included qualitative market research in the form of focus groups and in-depth one-on-one interviews. The first round of the research collected information on the disclosure forms that were being used by credit card issuers and the latter round exposed consumers to new disclosure forms and collected feedback. Using the feedback from the qualitative research, the Federal Reserve proposed revisions to Regulation Z and included proposed new disclosure forms. The Federal Reserve Board continued the evaluation of its proposed disclosure forms with additional rounds of testing.

The additional rounds of testing included in-depth interviews with consumers lasting 90 minutes each. Consumers were exposed to several mock disclosures. Three different types of credit card disclosures were tested.

1. Solicitation and application disclosures, where credit card terms were described in tabular form, often called the "Schumer Box" on the application, direct mail solicitation, or solicitation letter.
2. Periodic statement disclosures, where credit card terms are described in a monthly statement informing the consumer of the monthly payment amount, due date, and finance charge. The mock periodic statement disclosure also included changes to terms.

3. Convenience or balance transfer check disclosures, describing the terms of how consumers can access the credit account through checks.

The respondent or consumer read the mock disclosure and the interviewer asked the consumer to think out loud and describe what he or she thought. In order to evaluate the consumer's understanding of the disclosures the interviewer then asked a series of follow-up questions. The questions evaluated consumer awareness and understanding of the disclosures on the solicitation letter and application, periodic statement, and convenience checks. The follow-up questions assessed consumer understanding of the credit limit offered in the solicitation and whether the individual understood that he or she may not be approved for the full amount. The interviewer also explored whether consumers could correctly identify the APR and differentiate between the APR's offered for purchases and cash advances and balance transfers, introductory APR and its loss, penalty fees, payment allocation to different balances, grace period, late payment and minimum payment, payment changes, and other matters included in the mock solicitation letters, periodic statements, and convenience check offer.[8]

The Credit Card Responsibility and Disclosure Act calls upon the Federal Reserve to review the credit card market every 2 years. This mandatory review includes the terms of credit card agreements and practices of credit card issuers, the effectiveness of disclosures of terms, fees, and other expenses, and the adequacy of protections against unfair and deceptive acts and practices of credit card issuers.[9]

Although not explicitly required by the Credit Card Responsibility and Disclosure Act, monitoring the customer experience in the credit card marketplace can help determine whether the practices of credit card companies are fair and whether consumers are receiving appropriate information. Credit card companies at the same time can monitor their practices to ensure adherence to the law but also to ensure consumers are satisfied with their products and services in order to ensure customer loyalty and optimal customer acquisition. Certainly, government regulators and enforcement agencies, financial institutions and community groups can make use of well accepted market research methods to help ensure that credit card practices are fair and reasonable and facilitate appropriate consumer credit card decisions. Ongoing monitoring that uses mystery shopping, customer surveys, consumer panels, and focus groups can help ensure that the new requirements of the Credit Card Responsibility and Disclosure Act are being adhered to and provide adequate consumer protection.

5.2.2 Providian, Monitoring the Customer Experience to Ensure Complete Customer Satisfaction

In the credit card arena sales practices became increasingly aggressive in the late 1990s and continued to be aggressive into the new century. Using risk based scoring models credit card companies aggressively marketed their credit cards and ancillary products. These marketing and sales campaigns and the expansion into new and different product lines and delivery mechanisms fostered increased risk in an environment without adequate regulatory oversight.

The late 1990s and early 2000s witnessed cases where government enforcement agencies alleged that consumers faced deceptive credit card sales and marketing practices. In 2000 the Office of Comptroller of the Currency and Providian, a credit card company that operated a bank, agreed to a consent order whereby Providian placed $300 million into a deposit account designed to make restitution to consumers for misleading business, sales, and marketing practices. The allegations against Providian included unfair and deceptive practices in marketing credit cards and credit protection and not disclosing credit protection was limited to the number of months paid-in as well as several other restrictions. In addition, the allegations included unfair practices when processing payments in order to charge fees associated with late payments.

Among the allegations was the deception of marketing a no annual fee card and not disclosing that the purchase of credit protection for $156 per year was required to obtain the no fee card. Providian's solicitation letters did not prominently disclose the fact that the purchase of credit protection was mandatory for the "No Annual Fee" credit card. The application form did not disclose the fact that the purchase of credit protection was mandatory. Rather, Providian indicated that credit protection was included with the card.

When marketing credit protection Providian emphasized it was a great way to avoid making payments when hospitalized or when out of work. This leveraged financial security, a particular concern of low and moderate income consumers. However, Providian failed to disclose a number of limitations of credit protection coverage including:

1. The coverage was limited to the number of months the consumer paid in, even if that was less than the 18 months touted by the telemarketers.
2. Coverage was unavailable with regard to involuntary unemployment unless the consumer had paid in 3 months of premiums.

3. Coverage was unavailable with regard to involuntary unemployment if the consumer was self-employed.
4. Coverage was unavailable with regard to hospitalization, sickness, or disability caused by a pre-existing condition unless the consumer had paid in 6 months of premiums.
5. Coverage could be denied if the consumer paid more than the minimum to another credit card account beside Providian's.
6. It could be denied if the consumer accessed credit from a credit card other than the Providian card.

Still another allegation was that Providian deceived customers about a guaranteed savings rate associated with transferring balances to a Providian credit card without ever revealing the amount of the savings. Telemarketers followed scripts which avoided responding to potential customers who pressed for an answer to how much they would save. No matter how often the consumer questioned, the telemarketer, as directed by Providian, never told the consumer that the maximum saving over the rate the consumer had been paying was 0.7% in one rollout and 0.3% in another. Customers who were dissatisfied with the rate reduction had to pay 3% of the outstanding balance in order to transfer balances to another financial institution. And the customers had to prove to Providian's satisfaction within 90 days the interest rate they were previously paying in order to obtain the savings. If the customer did not provide acceptable information about the interest rate they were paying Providian would charge the maximum rate allowed under the account agreement, which was often 21.00%.

Providian also enticed consumers to open a credit card account through its "Real Check Program." The program offered a reward of $100 or $200 for opening an account but did not tell the customer he or she was required to transfer a minimum balance. In the case of the $200 reward, consumers were required to transfer a minimum balance of $10,000.

All allegations maintained Providian did not adequately disclose the features and restrictions of the programs it marketed. Still another allegation against Providian included not promptly recording the receipt of payments and thereby inappropriately charging late fees.

In addition to monetary restitution Providian agreed to change its policies and its telemarketing scripts to ensure that all fees, charges, and product limitations are fully and accurately disclosed to consumers before the purchase of any product. Providian also agreed to refrain from making any misleading or deceptive representations to consumers and to provide consumers with the right to cancel purchases up to 30 days after the first bill.[10]

All the alleged misleading and unfair marketing practices conducted by Providian are easily detected by ongoing monitoring of the sales and service process. Ongoing monitoring through mystery shopping and customer surveys could have prevented or limited the number of customers who were misled. In addition the costly and lengthy process of investigating and reaching settlement with Providian may have been avoided. Mystery shopping and customer surveys detect misleading sales practices, including failure to disclose and actions which mislead current and potential customers. Mystery shopping using carefully crafted scenarios and profiles will identify a pattern and practice which misleads or misinforms potential and current customers. Customer surveys will also identify issues associated with misleading practices and tardy processing of customer payments. However, the findings drawn from customer surveys are subject to the consumer's memory and perceptions. Nevertheless if consumers report they are not aware of key features and limitations of a credit card recently opened then the sales practices of the credit card issuer are called into question. In addition, if a substantial proportion of customers report late fees when payments are submitted on a timely basis then the timely processing of customer payments by the card issuer is subject to doubt and criticism.

As a result and after the agreement with the Office of the Comptroller of the Currency, Providian launched several initiatives and made changes to its sales and marketing practices. To ensure that these initiatives and sales and marketing practices were being executed the company employed several monitoring programs including call recordings, mystery shopping, customer satisfaction telephone surveys, and ongoing qualitative research.

5.2.2.1 Mystery Shopping

As part of its mystery shopping program Providian recruited cardholders to call its telephone representatives and measure the experience they encountered. The mystery callers made inquiries and conducted transactions and measured the information provided and whether scripts were adhered to. Unlike customer surveys which are retrospective and where consumers don't always accurately remember disclosures and information provided, mystery shopping provides a record of the treatment or experience encountered by the mystery shopper or tester. The mystery shops enabled Providian to measure whether the changes made to call scripts and policies concerning disclosures and information provided to consumers were being implemented. It enabled Providian to recognize employees for implementing the changes and for providing superior customer service, and to coach those employees that did not adhere to the changes. For example, at the end of all calls the telephone representatives were required to ask customers if they were completely satisfied.[11] The mystery shopping enabled the company to measure adherence to this protocol as well as others. At the same time the company instituted a call monitoring program whereby all calls were recorded to eliminate "slamming a practice whereby telemarketers sell unwanted services.[12]

5.2.2.2 Customer Satisfaction Telephone Surveys and Focus Groups

The company also sought feedback from its customers. A series of telephone based surveys were completed each quarter throughout the year to measure customer satisfaction with the company and elicit comments from its customers about its service and products. The company collected information from its cardholders in each of its credit card lines. Some of the information the company collected was:

- How satisfied customers were
- What customers liked and disliked
- Whether the customer called Providian recently and why
    - Whether the customer called about a problem and if it was resolved
    - Whether the customer called about a fee and the nature of the fee
    - How satisfied the cardholder was with the service provided during the call
- Impressions about the company's products and services
    - Whether the customer received a good value for the fees and rates paid,
    - If the company's terms were easy to understand,
    - If balance transfers were easy,
    - If the company's fees and rates were fair,
- Usage of ancillary products, e.g., credit protection
    - Satisfaction with the credit protection
- How Providian Compared to Other Credit Card Companies

The company used the program to detect customer problems and measure whether it was meeting customer needs. Problems voiced by its customers were then examined in light of its procedures and sales and marketing protocols and resolved on an ongoing basis.

6

MEASURING FAIR TREATMENT OF CONSUMERS IN THE INVESTMENT MARKETPLACE

Nearly half of all U.S. households own equities or bonds.[1] The volatility in the value of equities and bonds, and sharp downturns in the U.S. and world economies and employment situations during the years 2006 through 2009 has made the importance of managing and accounting for risk associated with asset volatility fundamental to sound financial decisions.

The U.S. Census estimates that by 2030 19% of the population will be 65 years of age or older versus 13% in 2008. Another 29% will be between 40 and 64 years of age versus 33% in 2008, and 52% will be less than 40 years of age as compared to 55% in 2008. The aging of the population will mean a shift in investment goals and objectives. More emphasis will be placed on investments that generate income, especially by consumers 65 years of age and older. This means consumer goals will be increasingly vulnerable to a volatile investment marketplace.

Equity and bond ownership is typically lower for non-White and lower income households, the groups that most need to build wealth. A little more than half of non-Hispanic White households (55%) own equities or bonds versus one-third (33%) of other households.[2] The increased fluctuation or volatility in asset values combined with increasingly complex financial instruments increases uncertainty among consumers and disproportionally impacts the consumers who are less comfortable with financial institutions and financial products; that is, minorities or non-White consumers.

Issues related to the ability of consumers to make proper investment decisions are compounded by the instability of financial markets and complexity of products. A telephone survey among a nationally projectable sample of 1,488 adults completed by the FINRA Investment Education Foundation in 2009[3] depicts a population that views its financial knowledge as high but yet is financially illiterate in many areas and less than capable of making correct financial decisions. The survey revealed that many consumers had difficulty answering questions about basic financial concepts. While prevalent across all groups, financial illiteracy disproportionally impacted females, those with lower income, and minorities. For example, one-third of the consumers surveyed could not correctly answer that money deposited in a savings account earning 1% interest during a year with 2% inflation would buy less (see Figure 6.1).

It is vitally important in this environment for consumers to be properly informed and offered suitable products based on investment objectives. Consumers armed with adequate investment information can better make optimal decisions regarding the allocation of funds between savings and investments and consumption. Adding to the risk concerns generated by the complexity and precariousness of the investment marketplace is the aging population. Senior citizens are more vulnerable to unstable markets and improper information and advice. Seniors have less time than younger consumers to recover from losses associated with making improper investment decisions and declining markets. A solid understanding of the features and benefits of investment and insurance products is necessary to help ensure optimal investment decisions relative to the risk offered. Critical to consumers being offered suitable investment products and having a solid understanding of investment products are employers, investment providers, and financial advisors.

Market research can help ensure that consumers have access to the information and products needed to make appropriate investment and savings decisions. It can assess whether products are offered based on a thorough understanding of the customer's needs, financial situation, and risk tolerance. In addition, it can verify whether racial profiling or gender bias affects the investment advice consumers receive. For the government the same market research approaches can be used to help set public policy and verify adherence to regulations and laws designed to help consumers make appropriate investment decisions. The surveys can help verify whether consumers are receiving appropriate information and if they understand the products being offered along with their benefits and risks.

A survey using mystery shoppers was conducted by *Money Magazine* in 1994. The magazine found that "brokers still treat men better

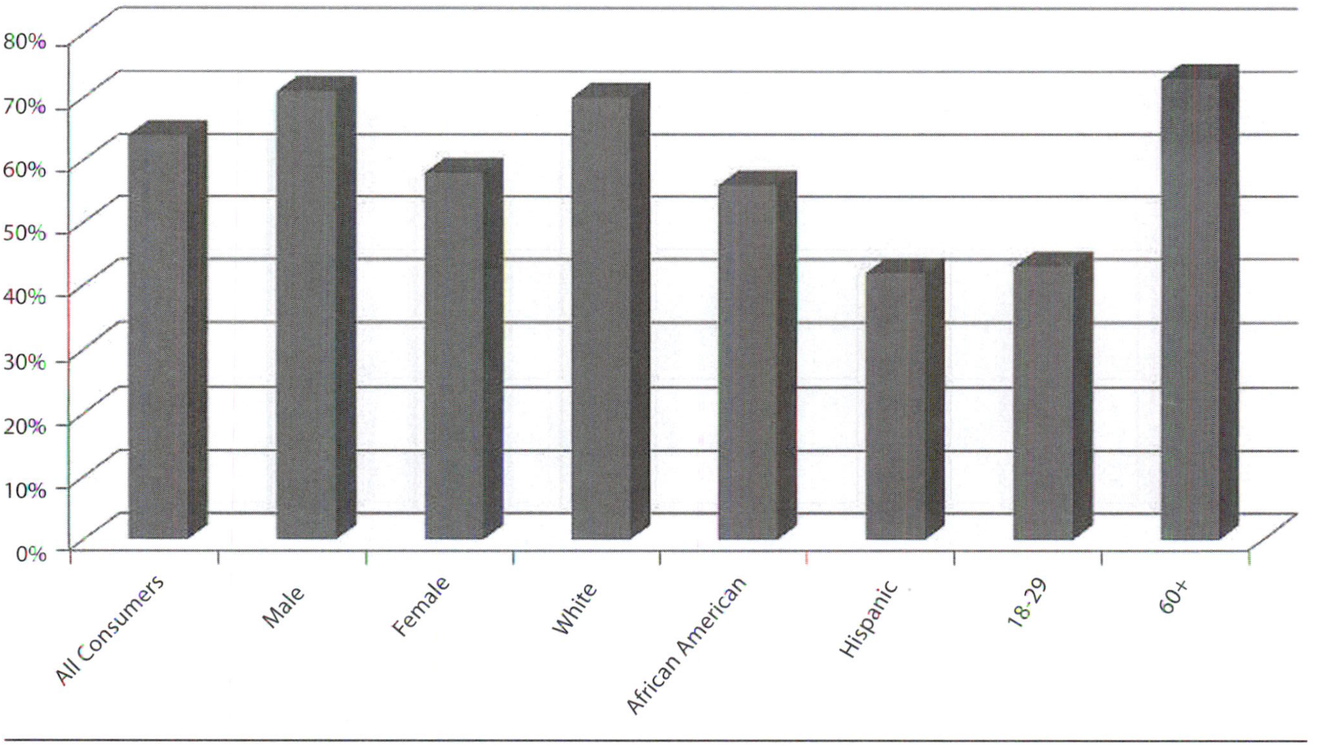

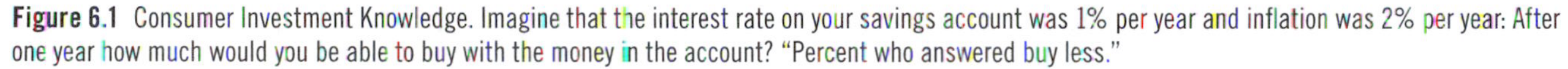

Figure 6.1 Consumer Investment Knowledge. Imagine that the interest rate on your savings account was 1% per year and inflation was 2% per year: After one year how much would you be able to buy with the money in the account? "Percent who answered buy less."

than women." The survey consisted of 100 mystery shops, 50 by men and 50 by women at six major brokerage firms. All had similar profiles and investment objectives. The results showed that brokers spent more time providing advice to men, offered a wider variety and higher risk investments to men, and tried harder to acquire men as customers. In addition, the level of service could have been better for both men and women. In 35% of the mystery shops brokers did not ask about the risk tolerance of the potential customers or mystery shoppers.[4] Certainly, gender bias and racial bias have no role to play in determining appropriate investment options for consumers.

However, brokerage firms and other investment providers (banks and insurance companies) are reliant on a network of specialized employees or independent agents who have discretion in terms of the products and advice offered and at times fees charged. Business cultures such as these are more prone to situations where sales and service representatives classify consumers into groups for easier decision making. Hence, women and minorities are assumed to be less knowledgeable and sophisticated about investments and to have smaller portfolios than males and Whites.

6.1 REGULATORY GUIDELINES CONCERNING THE SALE OF MUTUAL FUNDS AND NON-DEPOSIT INVESTMENT PRODUCTS

Unlike a brokerage firm or mutual fund company, a bank offers FDIC insured checking and savings accounts. Because of the availability of FDIC insured products, consumers place a high degree of trust in banks and view these institutions as places where they can safely deposit funds. In order to avoid confusion between deposit products that are FDIC insured and non-deposit investment products which are not FDIC insured, the bank regulatory agencies developed guidelines for the sale of non-deposit investment products at banks. The objective of the guidelines is to help ensure that consumers have a clear understanding of the nature of investment products and the differences between investments and deposit products. To do this the guidelines focus on the sales and application process. Specifically, guidelines were established concerning the sales setting, oral disclosures and suitability based questioning, products offered and recommended, fees quoted, distribution of prospectuses, and closing actions of the representative when meeting with prospective clients.

The guidelines issued by the four regulatory agencies (Office of the Comptroller of the Currency, Federal Reserve Board, Office of Thrift

Supervision, and Federal Deposit Insurance Corporation [FDIC]) specifically recommend a series of steps (inclusive of oral and written disclosures) aimed at ensuring that customers purchasing non-deposit investment products have a clear understanding of the nature of the products and the fact that they are not insured by the FDIC.

The interagency guidelines recommend the following disclosures when selling or advising consumers about non-deposit investment products at banks: (1) the fact that non-deposit investment products are not insured by the FDIC; (2) that non-deposit investment products are subject to risk and possible loss of the principal amount invested; and (3) that the money invested in these products are not deposits or other obligations of the institution and are not guaranteed by the institution. The interagency guidelines also hold that advertisements and brochures should clearly and conspicuously state these disclosures. Where applicable, the bank or depository institution needs to disclose the existence of an advisory relationship between the financial institution and an investment company whose shares are sold by the bank. Any relationship between the financial institution and affiliates providing or selling non-deposit investment products need to be discussed as well as any fees, penalties, or surrender charges.[5]

The interagency guidelines also recommend the disclosures take place in oral and written form during the pre-application and application stages of the investment process. The guidelines point out that the sales or branch environment should limit consumer confusion about the nature of non-deposit investment products and the role of FDIC insurance and the institution. Advertising and brochures for non-deposit investment products should be separate from deposit products, and the area where non-deposit investment products are sold should also be separate from the deposit-taking areas.

Banks involved in the sale of non-deposit investment products are also required to follow the rules of FINRA and the National Association of Securities Dealers (NASD), as set forth in "Rules Fair of Practice," and "Conduct Rules" and of the Office of the Comptroller of the Currency in OCC Bulletin 94-13. An investment representative and bank salesperson must ask sufficient needs-based questions (about income, financial and tax status, ownership, risk tolerance, goals, liquidity, and so on) to be able to make available or recommend suitable products. When selling mutual funds, representatives must discuss with the consumer all material facts related to the investment product. Before discussing the facts related to the investment the representative must determine whether the product is suitable for the consumer. The customer's financial and tax status should be explored along with their investment objectives, goals, time horizon, risk tolerance, and household income.

Banks must also limit the role of employees who are not properly licensed or trained in investment product sales (tellers and customer service representatives, for example). These employees should neither provide advice nor sell investment products. Their activities should be limited to mentioning the availability of non-deposit products and making referrals to properly trained representatives.

6.2 MARKET RESEARCH AND SELF-TESTING IN THE INVESTMENT MARKETPLACE

Traditional market research approaches, such as mystery shopping, consumer surveys, and focus groups are tools financial institutions traditionally use to limit risk associated with customer dissatisfaction and failure to meet customer needs. These market research approaches do this by verifying and measuring whether consumer needs are being met and whether or not consumers are receiving the information needed to make appropriate investment decisions. The same market research approaches can help financial institutions limit the legal and reputational risk associated with allegations of misleading sales practices, offering inappropriate products, and by measuring compliance with laws and guidelines concerning the sale of investments or non-deposit investment products. For the government, these approaches can help determine whether consumers are being served well and in a manner that serves the public well-being. Information gleaned from these studies can help guide public policy so as to ensure that the marketplace functions properly and serves to help consumers optimize their financial decisions.

6.2.1 Mystery Shopping and Investment Sales Practices

Mystery shopping can play a powerful role in helping financial institutions and the government verify that the investment marketplace is functioning properly. The technique identifies the sales practices encountered by consumers seeking to invest and whether it is of a nature which fosters appropriate investment decisions.

The mystery shop needs to be robust and not limited to measures of customer courtesy and friendliness. It needs to measure the questions asked, the products offered and recommended, the features and terms of the investment products discussed, and sales practices. The mystery shop program also needs to measure the performance of both commission and fee incented for sales personnel and third parties used by financial institutions to market products. Sales personnel must be monitored despite the fact that mystery shopping may take away from the time sales personnel spend with customers. The sales practices of third parties must be measured even though they are not employees. Not monitoring the sales practices encountered by consumers seeking to make investment product purchases permits an environment where misleading sales practices can occur. These practices can occur even though guidelines and training programs requiring the fair treatment of customers are put in place. Sales forces are too large and the life experiences and backgrounds and product knowledge of the sales personnel too varied to ensure appropriate treatment of customers without robust monitoring.

6.2.1.1 The Scenario

Mystery shoppers or testers posing as consumers may inquire on-site, over the telephone, or even via e-mail and the Internet about non-deposit investment products. Many scenarios include the testers mentioning their interest in investing money for a return higher than currently offered by certificates of deposit. Many times the testers ask questions of the representatives if the information is not volunteered. Two typical question shoppers ask are:

1. How secure is my money?
2. What rate of return can I expect?

Use of the scenario helps guarantee that shoppers will carry out the inquiry consistently and that representatives respond to the same inquiry. This helps ensure a reliable measure of whether or not consistent service is being offered to potential similarly situated customers across offices and representatives.

A typical scenario is shown in Figure 6.2.

6.2.1.2 The Profile

The testers use a profile containing information detailing the nature of the inquiry as well as the amount to invest, investment experience, investments currently owned, risk tolerance, household income, and occupation. Figure 6.3 describes a profile used by a tester or mystery

SAMPLE TESTER SCENARIO FOR AN INVESTMENT MYSTERY SHOP

Investment Inquiry

- Notice the time you enter the office and the time you leave the office.
- Make all required observations when you enter the office.
- Approach any available representative and ask to see someone about an investment.
- Keep track of the amount of time you spend waiting (if any) for the representative to become available to help you.
- Take note of any signs indicating investment products are offered and their location and whether or not they were in a deposit area of the branch or on the representative's desk that helped you.
- When you reach the representative who can help you with investment information, restate (if necessary) that **you want to get some information about an investment**.

If he/she asks what kind of investment you are interested in, say:

"I'm not sure. I want to see what you have available."

- If the representative asks you probing questions, respond as indicated on page 2 of this scenario and in your Shopper Profile.
- Listen carefully to everything the representative tells you about different types of investments. If you find it necessary to take notes, you may do so only in a manner that a normal customer would.
- Do **not** sign anything or fill out an application. Your goal is to get information.
- Listen for any discussion of:
  - Questions concerning your needs and financial circumstances
  - Types of investment products offered
  - Features and/or benefits of investment products
  - Fees
  - Rates of return
  - Mentions about insurance, FDIC Insurance and SIPC, potential risk and nature and role of the bank

Figure 6.2 Sample Tester Scenario for an Investment Mystery Shop

If the representative does not mention you must ask the following:

Product recommendation: "What do you recommend?"

Liquidity: "How easy is it to get my money or take my money out?"

Fees: "Are there fees?

Performance: "What will I earn?"

Funds required: "How much do I need to open my account? Is there a minimum?"

INVESTMENT INQUIRY GENERAL PROFILE	
Probing Question	**Response**
Your name?	Use a name other than your own, An "alias".
Your Social Security number? Your date of birth?	"I will give out that information if I decide to apply, right now I'm just trying to see what you have to offer."
Have you owned a home before?	"YES."
Your telephone number?	"I will be glad to give out that information if I decide to apply, but right now I'm just trying to see what you have to offer."
Where do you currently bank?	Name your own bank.
What type of investment are you interested in?	"I'm not sure. What are my options?"

See Shopper Profiles for specific information.

Upon completion of your inquiry, exit the office and drive away. Fill out the questionnaire after you are a few blocks away from the office. Write the office number and your interviewer number on the business card you have been given (if any). Staple the business card to the front page of the questionnaire.

Attach any brochures /applications/literature, etc. you received to the questionnaire. Write your interviewer number and office number on all materials received.

Figure 6.2 Continued

shopper. The profile can be used whether mystery shopping a bank, brokerage, or mutual fund company.

The research design can incorporate different tests and use different scenarios and profiles depending on the objective. For example, a bank or regulator may wish to evaluate whether appropriate investments are offered. The test can therefore be constructed to incorporate two different scenarios and profiles: (1) Determine whether more conservative, safer investment products are offered to seniors or older consumers, and (2) determine whether more aggressive, higher risk products are offered to younger consumers and to investigate whether males and females receive the same information.

SAMPLE TESTER PROFILE FOR AN INVESTMENT MYSTERY SHOP

Amount to Invest	$300,000
Objective	Save for retirement
Risk Tolerance	Conservative but willing to accept some risk for growth
Investment experience	Some, a 401k at work invested in mutual funds, some mutual funds and CD's
Source of funds	Inheritance and rollover CD
Investment Assets	$170,000 consisting of 401K $100,000, CD's $30,000, Mutual Funds $40,000
Age	55
Gender	Male
Occupation	Work at a large employer in area. Work in procurement or another area shopper is comfortable with
Marital status	Married
Household Income	$130,000 per year Shopper $90,000 per year Spouse $40,000
Tax bracket	28%
Home Ownership	Yes
Home Value	$300,000 (based on area)
Mortgage Outstanding	$150,000
Credit card debt	$200 per month
Auto loan debt	$250 per month

Figure 6.3 Sample Tester Profile for an Investment Mystery Shop

6.2.1.2.1 PROFILE 1

Mystery shoppers 55 to 60 years of age pose as potential customers preparing for retirement and about to pay college expenses. Here, the end user is evaluating whether the mystery shopper is asked appropriate questions and offered products suitable to their financial goals, risk tolerance, and liquidity needs. Of particular concern would be offering and recommending equity products carrying risk or annuity products where the money is not accessible for a fixed period of time.

6.2.1.2.2 PROFILE 2

Male and female mystery shoppers 35 to 45 years with $100,000 seek to invest for growth and have no immediate liquidity needs. They may need to access some of the money in 10 years when their children attend college and the remainder upon retirement. Of particular interest is whether the male and female shoppers are offered similar products, asked similar questions, and given similar information. A concern might be offering a fixed annuity product and not mutual funds; for example, a large cap growth mutual fund.

The mystery shoppers do not fill out any paperwork but only gather information on the customer experience and the information provided. Once a conversation with a bank employee is finished, the tester completes a questionnaire describing the experience and his or her impressions.

6.2.1.3 The Questionnaire

The questionnaire consists of a series of yes/no questions pertaining to the sales environment, needs based discovery, product information and products made available, note taking and the use of a computer, fees quoted, discussion of returns and historical performance, efforts to close the sale, and tester impressions including overall satisfaction. Attention is normally paid to offering suitable products, understanding potential customer investment objectives, risk tolerance. and liquidity need, and how historical performance is related to future performance, and any pressure tactics used during the sales presentation or discussion with the representative. Pressure tactics might involve using unrealistic price appreciation tied to a need to invest now or lose the chance to invest, telling stories of a similarly situated consumer that didn't invest with the representative and is now without adequate funds for retirement, or offering false credentials to build credibility and trust. Figure 6.4 describes the most popular topics covered in a questionnaire mystery shoppers use to record their experiences.

MYSTERY SHOPPER NON-DEPOSIT INVESTMENT QUESTIONNAIRE TOPICS

- Time entered and left location
- Did the person who greeted you refer you to someone else to help you with your inquiry?
- What was the title of the person who helped you?
- What was the gender of the person who helped you?
- During your meeting with the representative that helped you, did he or she:
  - Ask for your name
  - Address you by name
  - Introduce himself or herself
  - Smile
  - Offer you a seat
  - Shake your hand
  - Thank you
- How did the person who helped you describe his or her relationship with the bank?
  - Employee of the bank
  - Employee of a third party
  - Other (specify)
- Were there any FDIC signs or deposit product signs on the representative's desk or the area where you met with the representative?
- Was there a SIPC (Securities Investment Protection Corporation) sign on the representative's desk or the area where you met with the representative?
- During you meeting with the representative did he or she mention:
  - Investment products are not FDIC insured
  - Investment products are subject to investment risk, including possible loss of principal invested
  - Investment products are not deposits or obligations of the bank and are not guaranteed by the bank
- If the representative mentioned investment products are not FDIC insured, are subject to risk and are not deposits of or guaranteed by the bank did he or she do so before or after offering and recommending a product?
- Were you asked any of the following questions
  - What you want to do with the money?
  - When you will need the money?
  - How long you want to invest the money?
  - How much risk you are willing to accept?
  - How much experience do you have investing?
  - What type of investments do you own?
  - The value of your investment assets and savings?

  - How much debt you have?
  - What your household income is?
  - What your tax bracket is?
  - Whether you have a 401K or IRA?
  - Whether you own a home?
  - How old you are?
  - Do you have children and their ages?
- What types of products were mentioned, explained and recommended?
- Did the representative offer a prospectus and for which products?
- Did the representative discuss fees? If so what types of fees were discussed?
- Did the representative:
  - Ask you to open an account today?
  - Attempt to schedule an appointment to open the account?
  - Ask for your telephone number so he or she could follow-up?
- How satisfied (Extremely Satisfied, Very Satisfied, Somewhat Satisfied, Neither Satisfied or Dissatisfied, Somewhat Dissatisfied, Very Dissatisfied, Extremely Dissatisfied) were you with the representative and:
  - The overall service he or she provided?
  - His or her product knowledge?
  - The responsiveness to your request?
  - The ease of understanding the information provided?
  - The courtesy he or she provided?
  - His or her ability to understand your needs?
  - His or her organization?
  - His or her acting as a trusted financial advisor?
- If you were Somewhat Dissatisfied, Very Dissatisfied or Extremely Dissatisfied with the overall service please describe why.
- At any time during the conversation did you feel pressured by the representative?
  - If yes, why?

Figure 6.4 Mystery Shopper Non-deposit Investment Questionnaire Topics

6.2.1.4 The Report

The data must be reported to meet or answer the objective of the research; to assess whether the financial institution's sales practices convey a clear understanding about the nature of non-deposit investment products. When using mystery shopping to measure and help ensure adherence to government agency regulatory guidelines and the law, results are reviewed at the total or corporate level and then by region, district, and representative levels.

Special attention is given to the oral disclosures, suitability based questioning and products offered, the sales setting, and whether it is conducive to a clear understanding about the differences between deposit products (e.g., checking and savings accounts) and non-deposit investment products). The percentage of potential customers ("mystery shoppers") who are told and not told non-deposit products are not FDIC insured, are not deposits or obligations of the bank, and involve risk and possible loss of principal, is reviewed along with the questions asked by the representatives and whether products were offered based on an understanding of the potential customer's needs and profile. This tells the financial institution whether its corporate practices are of a nature that ensures a clear understanding of investment products and the risk associated with sales practices that do not convey a clear understanding of these products. For example, it may find that its sales and service process limits upfront discussion about investment products and relies solely on oral and written disclosures during the account opening.

Figure 6.5 shows how a financial institution may view adherence to inter-agency guidelines concerning oral disclosures. The results shown in Figure 6.5 indicate that a substantial proportion of potential customers are probably not being informed about the nature of non-deposit investment products and the role of the financial institution. As a first

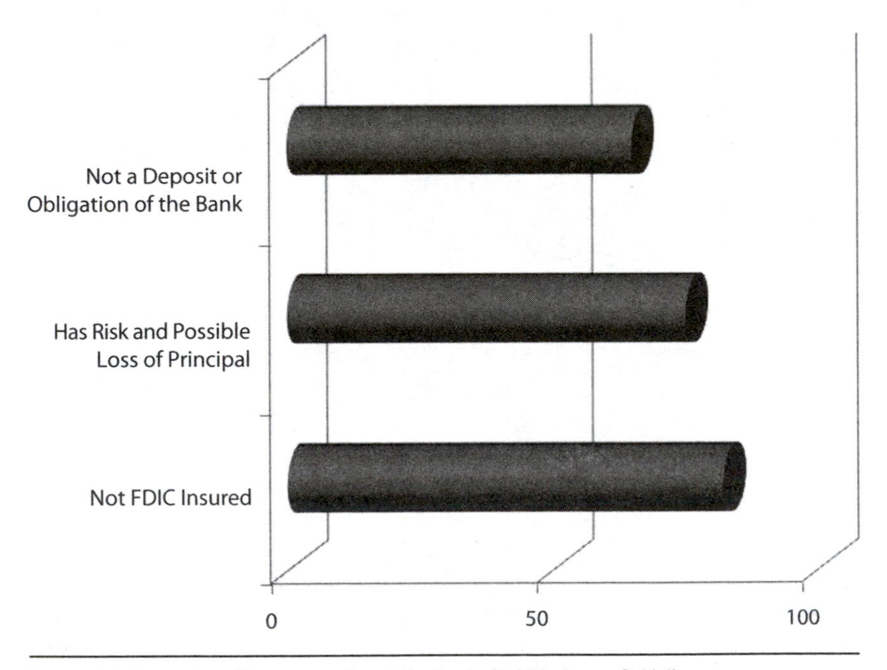

Figure 6.5 Proportion of Representatives Adhering to Oral Disclosure Guidelines

step the financial institution can provide feedback to its representatives concerning the results and query the representatives about the cause. The financial institution might find that some of its representatives were concerned they would scare potential customers and lose business and therefore waited to make the disclosures during the account opening. The financial institution undertook re-training of its investment representatives with particular emphasis on the inter-agency guidelines and the importance of adherence to ensure customers understand the nature of investment products and role of the institution during the pre-application sales process. The financial institution set standards and defined the process by which potential customers are served. A clear policy was set concerning the inter-agency guidelines and goals were established and communicated to regional managers and representatives. The financial institution also informed representatives and their managers how adherence to the financial institution's sales and service standards would be monitored and enforced.

The findings in Figure 6.5 have implications for public policy. Even though the government regulators have issued guidelines to help foster a clear understanding of the nature of investment products and the role of the bank, a substantial proportion of potential customers are not receiving the oral disclosures and are probably confused about the products being sold. Consideration might be given to issuing regulations concerning the sale of investment products at banks or more rigorous oversight of the sales process.

6.2.1.5 The Report Cards

It is particularly important to generate report cards that describe the experience encountered by the mystery shoppers with each representative. This permits the financial institution to take action with specific representatives if needed. For example, further training or disciplinary action may be required in cases where clear violations of policy have occurred combined with other issues (customer complaints).

Specific representatives that are adhering and not adhering to the inter-agency guidelines are identified and the financial institution provides feedback to representatives describing their performance. Financial institutions may elect to set clear policy standards concerning adherence to inter-agency guidelines and non-deposit investment product sales practices and remedial efforts and penalties associated with non-adherence. Some bank policy standards have in fact clearly explained that non-adherence to interagency guidelines may result in termination.

6.2.2 Consumer Surveys and Investment Sales Practices

In addition to assessing whether or not consumer needs are being met, consumer surveys monitor whether consumers understand the nature of investment products and the role of the financial institution. The surveys provide consumers with a venue for speaking with the financial institution about what they dislike and like about the financial institution and the products offered and purchased. While many financial institutions monitor consumer complaints, there are many consumers that do not directly contact the financial institution about their concerns and complaints. Consumer surveys provide a venue for both the consumer and the financial institution to communicate. As such the consumer can voice their concerns and the financial institution can respond to resolve the concern and correct issues and thereby improve customer satisfaction.

Financial institutions may elect not to survey recent customers about their understanding of investment products out of a fear for raising undue concerns among customers and complaints. For the past several years many regulators and examiners have deferred to the financial institutions and suggested monitoring complaints in lieu of surveying recent customers. This approach is short sighted and may in fact perpetuate sales practices that do not foster a clear understanding of the nature of investment products and the role of the financial institution.

6.2.2.1 Mail Surveys

The surveys are cost effective, provide a framework for thoughtful input, and provide customers with a sense of comfort associated with knowing the survey is from the bank or financial institution and that the consumer can provide the information in private. The mail, however, typically elicits a lower cooperation rate than other methods—10 to 25%. A key point to consider is whether the consumers who respond to the mail survey are likely to have the same opinions and attitudes as those who do not respond. If the answer is yes, then the data gathered from the respondents returning questionnaires should be representative of the population. Another key point to consider is timing. Mail surveys typically take longer owing to the time it takes to mail questionnaires, mail reminders to complete and return questionnaires, and then receive the completed questionnaires. This is particularly important if the purpose is to obtain feedback describing the experience the consumer encountered when he or she recently purchased an investment product. In this regard it is best to contact and interview consumers as soon as possible after the purchase.

6.2.2.2 Telephone Surveys

Telephone surveys still offer the most representative samples and provide the researcher with the ability to not only quantify information such as consumer awareness and agreement about product features, benefits, and attitudes but also probe into the reason for a consumer's dislikes, likes, and beliefs or actions. The ability to probe and clarify consumer responses during the telephone interview is a key strength of the procedure. Surveys of recent purchasers of investment products normally use customer lists with telephone numbers to randomly select customers to interview. Cooperation rates have declined recently in step with consumer concern for privacy and issues related to telemarketing. Using a customer list and providing the bank's name at the beginning of the survey and keeping the interview short helps to ensure cooperation.

6.2.2.3 Web Surveys

The use of the Internet or the Web to conduct research continues to grow. Many panels of consumers exist to conduct Internet-based research. The Internet panels are particularly helpful for general population surveys and surveys targeted at hard-to-reach consumers, such as doctors or other busy professionals. They fall short when the institution requires information from recent product purchasers or branch-based service since most financial institutions do not have accurate and sufficient numbers of customer e-mail addresses. Similar to mail surveys, Internet surveys do not permit an interviewer to probe and clarify questions. These surveys typically are not conducive to top of mind responses. Rather they permit the respondent to think about responses and even refer to outside sources for their responses. Lastly, issues related to non-response and in particular responses from the elderly are a concern. It is this group that represents the most risk to the institution in terms of not understanding the nature of investment products and the role of the bank. The elderly are the most likely to confuse investment products offered through a bank with deposit products that are FDIC insured.

6.2.2.4 Personal and Exit Surveys

The surveys are normally conducted in a branch or when a customer leaves a branch. They can also be conducted in a shopping mall setting. The branch-based interviews are particularly helpful for targeting customers of a branch and gathering information about the branch experience when it is fresh in the customer's mind. These surveys are subject to bias, however, in that branch employees know consumers are being surveyed and may alter their sales practices during the days consumers are being interviewed. In addition, the branch and shopping mall surveys only represent the consumers visiting the branch or mall that day, hence, the data user needs to assume that consumers who visited the branch or shopping mall that day will provide the same information as those that did not.

6.2.2.5 The Consumer Survey Questionnaire

The survey or questionnaire collecting responses from recent purchasers of an investment product are normally short, 10 minutes or less, and ascertain the consumer's experience and understanding of the nature of investment products and the role of the bank. The survey questions are crafted so as not to raise concerns among investors about the risk associated with the investment product or its features or benefits. As such, the survey normally avoids asking whether the customer was informed about specific features of the investment product and the specific role of the institution. Rather, the survey asks the respondent to rate their overall experience, what they disliked and liked, and whether they agree or disagree with statements describing the service, the product, the representative, and the role of the bank. Some surveys ask the customer's permission to inform the financial institution about the customer's dissatisfaction in order to contact the customer and resolve the issue. Figure 6.6 describes the topics normally covered in the questionnaire.

NON-DEPOSIT INVESTMENT PRODUCT CONSUMER SURVEY QUESTIONNAIRE TOPICS

- Overall how satisfied were you with the service you received? Were you Extremely Satisfied, Very Satisfied, Somewhat Satisfied, Neither Satisfied or Dissatisfied, Somewhat Dissatisfied, Very Dissatisfied or Extremely Dissatisfied?
- What did you dislike?
- What did you like?
- Do you agree or disagree with the following statements about investment products, e.g. mutual funds, stocks and bonds? Do you Completely Agree, Strongly Agree, Somewhat Agree, Neither Agree or Disagree, Somewhat Disagree, Strongly Disagree or Completely Disagree with:
  - Investment products, e.g. mutual funds, stocks and bonds are not covered by FDIC insurance

  - Investment products, e.g. mutual funds, stocks and bonds involve risk and the possible loss of principal
  - Investment products, e.g. mutual funds, stocks and bonds are not deposits or obligations of a bank
  - The past performance of investment products is no guarantee of future results
- Do you agree or disagree with the following statements describing the service provided by the representative who helped you? Do you Completely Agree, Strongly Agree, Somewhat Agree, Neither Agree or Disagree, Somewhat Disagree, Strongly Disagree or Completely Disagree with:
  - The representative asked questions to understand your needs
  - The representative was knowledgeable
  - The representative described his or her role
  - The representative clearly explained the features of the product
  - The representative clearly explained the fees
  - The representative acted as a trusted financial advisor
  - The representative did not pressure you to invest
  - The representative was courteous
- During your meeting with the representative did he or she describe his or her role or relationship with the bank?
- If yes, did he or she mention they were:
  - An employee of a third party and not a bank employee?
  - An employee of the bank? or
  - Something else? (please describe)
- How likely are you to recommend the representative to a friend or business associate? Are you, Definitely Likely, Very Likely, Somewhat Likely, Neither Likely or Unlikely, Somewhat Unlikely, Very Unlikely or Definitely Unlikely?
  - If Somewhat Unlikely, Very Unlikely or Definitely Unlikely, Why?
- In the future, how likely are you to use the representative for your investment needs? Are you, Definitely Likely, Very Likely, Somewhat Likely, Neither Likely or Unlikely, Somewhat Unlikely, Very Unlikely or Definitely Unlikely?
  - If Somewhat Unlikely, Very Unlikely or Definitely Unlikely, Why?
- Classification questions
  - Age
  - Gender
  - Income
- Is there anything else you would like to suggest or add concerning the service you recently received?
- Mr/Ms (read customer's name) you indicated you were dissatisfied with the overall service you received. With your permission may we inform (read the financial institution's name) about your dissatisfaction so someone can call you?

Figure 6.6 Non-deposit Investment Product Consumer Survey Questionnaire Topics

6.2.2.6 *The Consumer Survey Report*

The data collected must be reported to meet the objective of the research. In the case of a consumer survey designed to assess the effectiveness of compliance with interagency guidelines pertaining to the sale of non-deposit investment products, the report needs to quantify the degree of consumer understanding about the nature of investment products and the role of the bank. The report needs to indicate the percentage of consumers that properly understand the nature of these products and their features. It must also measure the percentage of customers that correctly understand the role of the bank in these products. Figure 6.7 describes how results are portrayed to communicate whether or not customers understand the nature of non-deposit products and the role of the bank.

The data reported in Figure 6.7 suggest confusion among a substantial proportion of recent purchasers. One out of five recent purchasers do not highly agree that investment products are not FDIC insured, involve risk, and that past performance does not guarantee future results. About half of those surveyed do not highly agree that investments are not obligations of the bank. The implication is that a substantial proportion of customers feel the value of their investment is secure when it is not. These recent purchasers may in fact complain should the investment lose value. More importantly these recent purchasers may have elected to invest the money in another investment vehicle had they understood the investment could decline in value.

Given these results steps need to be taken to ensure that recent purchasers have a clear understanding of the investment products purchased. A thorough review of what representatives verbally disclose to potential customers and the literature potential customers receive needs to be performed. The timing of the verbal and written descriptions is also reviewed. The review should also include in-depth interviews with recent purchasers and representatives. The in-depth interviews trace the sales process and the oral and written disclosures. Recent purchasers and representatives are asked where the process breaks down in terms of providing an accurate understanding of investment products. Once the areas where the process breaks down are identified the financial institution can institute changes.

The report should also describe customer concerns in a manner such that the financial institution can act to resolve issues that will limit the financial institution's risk associated with claims of misleading investment sales practices. Figure 6.8 describes some typical concerns that might be voiced by recent purchasers of investment products.

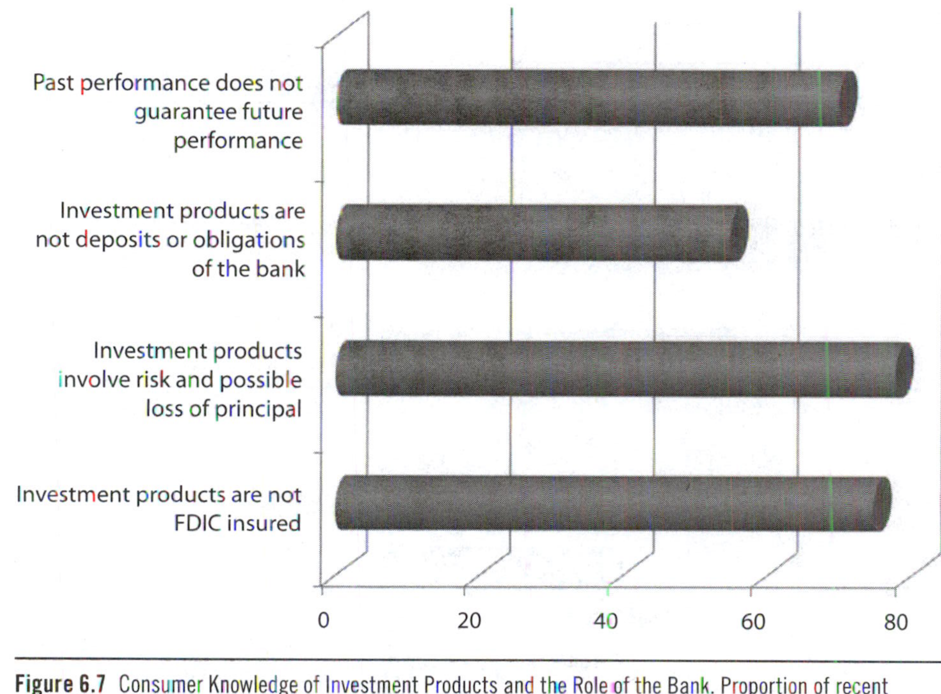

Figure 6.7 Consumer Knowledge of Investment Products and the Role of the Bank. Proportion of recent purchasers who strongly agree with statements describing investment products and the role of the bank.

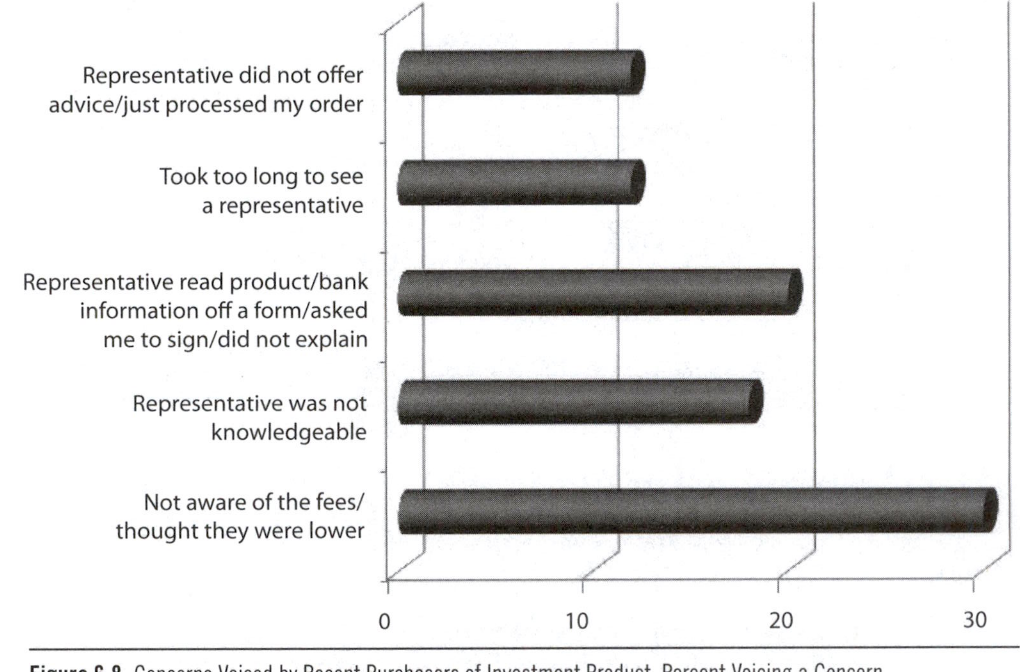

Figure 6.8 Concerns Voiced by Recent Purchasers of Investment Product, Percent Voicing a Concern

The data described in Figure 6.8 suggest a significant proportion of recent customers do not fully understand the fees associated with the investment product recently purchased. In addition, a substantial number claimed that the representatives simply read to them off a form regarding the product purchased and the role of the bank and didn't explain what it meant, and then asked the customer to sign a form stating that the disclosures have been read to them at the time of the product purchase and account opening. The implication is that the bank is not always informing customers about the nature of the product purchased, its fees, and the role of the bank as required by the interagency statement concerning the sale of non-deposit investment products and the Financial Industry Regulatory Authority (FINRA) rules of fair practice. In addition requiring customers to sign a form stating product disclosures have been made appears to be executed without adequate explanation, which leads to customer confusion. Such a policy is in the best interest of the financial institution, in that the financial institution can produce the form when the customer alleges he or she was misled.

The financial institution could remedy the issues by undertaking additional training with representatives as well as examining the sales and new account opening process to better understand why a substantial proportion of customers are saying the representatives are not explaining the disclosure forms.

For the government the findings of the consumer survey suggest that more emphasis needs to be placed on the sales process by regulators to ensure customers understand the investment products they are purchasing.

7
EPILOGUE

The financial services sector plays an intrinsic role in the well-being of the consumer and the nation. Recent history has shown that the marketplace does not and should not serve as the mechanism for preventing and correcting unfair and unsound business practices. The marketplace does not ensure the free and uninhibited flow of information and products, it is imperfect. Blacks and Hispanics and other minorities seeking credit may be treated differently from similarly situated Whites. Females may not always receive the information needed to make appropriate investment decisions. Consumers, regardless of race or gender, may be misled and steered to buying inappropriate products because companies and sales persons stand to make commissions or garner fees.

Programs which monitor the customer experience need to be conducted by individual financial institutions and the government. The programs will help ensure the marketplace is working, that consumers are treated fairly, and have adequate access to the information required to make appropriate financial decisions.

There are many reasons to monitor the customer experience. Financial well-being is one reason. Consumers who are not permitted access to appropriate financial products, who are misled or not given the information to make appropriate credit and investment decisions, risk purchasing the wrong product, which can have a profound impact on their financial security, wealth, and ultimately the health of the economy.

Ethics is another reason. Tactics that mislead or treat consumers unfairly or differently because of their race, national origin, age, or gender should be abhorred by society and financial institutions alike.

Legal liability is yet another reason to monitor. Companies are exposed to huge liabilities due to allegations of unfair treatment. In 2000 Providian paid $300 million to settle claims of unfair treatment of its customers. Citigroup in 2002 paid $215 million to settle allegations that the Associates, a company it acquired, engaged in systematic and widespread deceptive and abusive lending practices.

Fortunately, there are time tested self-testing and monitoring programs that can help ensure the marketplace is functioning properly. The use of these programs can help guide public policy to support and correct imperfections in the marketplace. Financial institutions can use the same approaches to ensure sound business practices which foster revenues and shareholder value. The consumer benefits, the financial institution benefits, and the nation benefits from these approaches.

NOTES

CHAPTER 2

1. John Baugh, NPR Morning Edition, September 5, 2001; and "Linguistic Profiling: Pilot Studies on Restaurants, Car Dealerships and Apartment Rentals," Kedami Fisseha, Nicolas Yannuzzi, January 12, 2007. Retrieved from http://www.scribd.com/doc/56957/Linguistic-Profiling-Pilot-Studies-on-Restaurants-Car-Dealerships-And-Apartment-Rentals
2. The Boston Federal Reserve, April 1992, *Closing the Gap: A Guide to Equal Opportunity Lending* and *Mortgage Lending In Boston: Interpreting HMDA Data*, October 1992.

CHAPTER 4

1. Extracted from testing conducted by Barry Leeds & Associates and the author in the early to mid-1990s.
2. *All Other Things Being Equal: A Paired Testing Study of Mortgage Lending Institutions*, The Urban Institute,Lanham, MD, April 2002, p.i.
3. Barry Leeds & Associates and Paul Lubin, *Fair Lending Testing Progress Report,* 1998, New York, NY; Author.
4. *Mortgage Lending, Racial Discrimination and Federal Policy,* Urban Institute Press, Washington, DC,1996, p. 612.
5. Senate Committee on Small Business and Entrepreneurship, testimony from Jon S. Wainwright, Ph.D., Vice President, NERA Economic Consulting, Concerning the Current State of Minority-Owned and Women-Owned Business Enterprises in the United States, May 22, 2007. Retrieved from http://www.nera.com/Publication.asp?p_ID=3148
6. Paul Lubin, "Fair Lending, Testing, Training and Best Practices," paper presented at the Understanding Consumer Credit Symposium, Joint Center for Housing Studies, Harvard University, Cambridge, MA, November 2007, p. 23.
7. *All Other Things Being Equal: A Paired Testing Study of Mortgage Lending Institutions*, The Urban Institute, Washington, DC, April 2002, p. iii.
8. Ibid., p. v.
9. Comptroller of Currency, Administrator of National Banks, AL 2002-3 Advisory

Letter Subject: Guidance on Unfair or Deceptive Acts or Practices Date: March 22, 2002, p. 2. Washington, DC: U.S. Department of Treasury.

10. FEDERAL TRADE COMMISSION, PLAINTIFF, v. Civil No. CITIGROUP INC., CITIFINANCIAL CREDIT COMPANY, ASSOCIATES FIRST CAPITAL CORPORATION, and ASSOCIATES CORPORATION OF NORTH AMERICA, Delaware corporations, COMPLAINT FOR PERMANENT INJUNCTION AND OTHER EQUITABLE RELIEF.
11. Erick Bergquist, *American Banker*, June 24, 2002 , "Too Much Information? Citi Mystery Shop Sparks Debate." Retrived from http://www.americanbanker.com/issues/167_122/-176032-1.html
12. House Financial Services Committee on Financial Institutions and Consumer Credit, Subcommittee Regarding Abusive Mortgage Lending Practices, Exotic Mortgages, and Foreclosures, Testimony of the National Community Reinvestment Coalition, Josh Silver, Vice President of Research and Policy, Tuesday, March 27, 2007.
13. Ibid.
14. Fair Housing Center of Greater Boston (May 2006), *The Gap Persists* (pp. 10–13). Author.
15. Silver, same as 12 above.
16. Fair Lending Testing, Training and Best Practices 1991–2007, Understanding Consumer Credit Symposium, Joint Center for Housing Studies, February 2008 and Market Research for Detecting and Eliminating Racial Profiling and Discrimination in Lending, American Marketing Association Public Policy Conference, May 2009.

CHAPTER 5

1. Nilson Report, April 2009.
2. U.S. Congress, Joint Economic Committee, "Vicious Cycle: How Unfair Credit Card Company Practices Are Squeezing Consumers and Undermining the Recovery," May 2009.Retrieved from http://www.creditcards.com/credit-card-news/credit-card-industry-facts-personal-debt-statistics-1276.php
3. *Credit Cards' Rising Interchange Fees Have Increased Costs for Merchants, but Options for Reducing Fees Pose Challenges*, Government Accounting Office, November 2009, p. 5.
4. American Bankers Association/Dove Consulting, *2005/2006 Study of Consumer Payment Preferences*. Washington, DC: Author, October 2005.
5. Center for Responsible Learning, CRL Research Brief, Washington, DC, April 2008.
6. Federal Reserve System 12 CFR Part 205[Regulation E; Docket No. R-1343] Electronic Fund Transfers, p. 8.
7. Regulation Z, 6500-Consumer Protection, Subpart B – Open End Credit, fdic.gov/regulations/laws/rules
8. *Designing and Testing of Effective Truth in Lending Disclosure, Findings from Qualitative Consumer Research*, submitted to Board of Governors of the Federal Reserve System, December 15, 2008, Macro International, Inc., Calverton, MD

9. Credit Card Responsibility and Disclosure Act, May 2009, H.R.627, www.gov-trak.us
10. Comptroller of the Currency Administrator of National Banks, Washington, DC, Fact Sheet, June 28, 2000 p. 36.
11. Jennifer Kingson and Lavonne Kuykendall, *American Banker,* June 12, 2001, "Providian Trumpets Image Makeover." Retrieved from, http://www.american-banker.com/issues/166_112/-151692-1.html
12. *USA Today,* "Providian Bounces Back with Revamped Strategy for Customer Service," May 8, 2001.

CHAPTER 6

1. *Financial Capability in the United States,* FINRA Investor Education Foundation, Washington, DC, December 2009.
2. *Equity and Bond Ownership in America*, 2008, Investment Company Institute and Security and Financial Markets Association, Washington, DC.
3. *Financial Capability,* December 2009.
4. "How to Find a Stockbroker You Can Really Trust." *Money Magazine*, August 1994. Retrieved from http://money.cnn.com/magazines/moneymag/moneymag_archive/1994/08/01/89048/index.htm
5. *Interagency Statement on Retail Sales of Non-Deposit Investment Products,* Retrieved from www.fdic.gov/regulations/rules/5000-4500.html#fdic5000interagencysor

INDEX

Page numbers in italics refer to figures or tables.

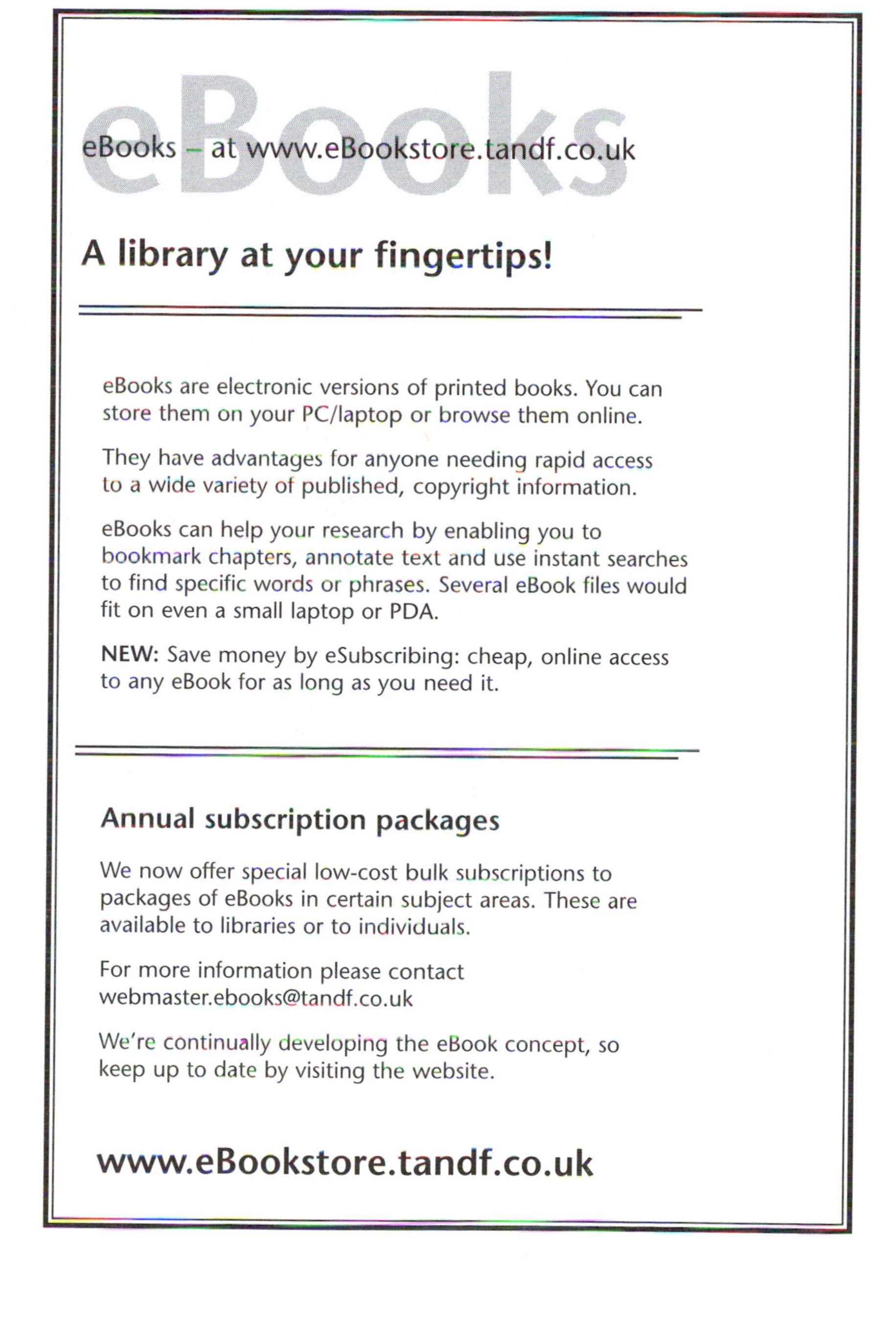
eBooks
eBooks – at www.eBookstore.tandf.co.uk
A library at your fingertips!
eBooks are electronic versions of printed books. You can store them on your PC/laptop or browse them online.
They have advantages for anyone needing rapid access to a wide variety of published, copyright information.
eBooks can help your research by enabling you to bookmark chapters, annotate text and use instant searches to find specific words or phrases. Several eBook files would fit on even a small laptop or PDA.
NEW: Save money by eSubscribing: cheap, online access to any eBook for as long as you need it.
Annual subscription packages
We now offer special low-cost bulk subscriptions to packages of eBooks in certain subject areas. These are available to libraries or to individuals.
For more information please contact webmaster.ebooks@tandf.co.uk
We're continually developing the eBook concept, so keep up to date by visiting the website.
www.eBookstore.tandf.co.uk